What Are They Saying About the Theology of Suffering?

Lucien Richard, O.M.I.

PAULIST PRESS
New York/Mahwah, N.J.

Library of Congress Cataloging-in-Publication Data

Richard, Lucien.
        What are they saying about the theology of suffering? by Lucien Richard.
            p.   cm.
        ISBN 0-8091-3347-4 (paper)
            1. Suffering—Religious aspects—Christianity—History of doctrines—20th century.   I. Title.
BT732. 7.R545   1992   92-21583
231' .8—dc20   CIP

Published by Paulist Press
997 Macarthur Boulevard
Mahwah, New Jersey 07430

Printed and bound in the
United States of America

Contents

For Alex and Teddy

My ability to bring this book to completion owes a special debt to two persons: Theresa Busher who typed and retyped the text, and Eleanor Morissey who edited the text.

Introduction

Suffering is a universal and most common experience for human beings. No one escapes it and, as such, suffering functions as a common denominator. Yet as universal and common as suffering is, it is also the one experience that is most personal and existential. Suffering leads to the fundamental questions about the self: Why me? Why do things always go wrong in my life? Why live? While common and universal, suffering causes a sense of isolation in the sufferer. The personal and existential nature of suffering expresses itself as victimization. Suffering also has an objectivity that is historical which characterizes human life on such a massive scale that it often defies thought.

While suffering in all of its forms is present in the human condition, the real anguish of suffering is found in its perceived meaninglessness. More than twenty-five hundred years ago, a man named Job stood under the curse of meaninglessness. He could not find a reason or a purpose for his suffering. The suffering of children is a particularly painful expression of meaninglessness. Humanity cries out for its elimination. There is so much innocent and meaningless suffering that no easy interpretation of suffering is possible. History presents itself to us as a mixture of meaning and meaninglessness, of sorrow and happiness. Such a mixture raises the question whether, in the last resort, we can trust life at all. The quest to find meaning in our life is our primary motivational force.

According to Viktor Frankl, the frustration of an individual's quest for meaning results in a certain type of neurosis which he has labeled "noogenic neurosis," i.e. a neurosis that is brought about by an

1

unrewarded search for meaning.[1] Meaning-making is a central human activity. According to Clifford Geertz, it is also the central function of a culture, for culture can be viewed as "the structures of meaning through which men give shape to their experience."[2] The same author understands religion to function as a cultural system. Religion is "a system of symbols which acts to establish powerful, pervasive and long-lasting moods and motivations in men by formulating conceptions or a central order of existence and clothing these conceptions with such an aura of factuality that the moods and motivations seem uniquely realistic."[3]

Suffering and Religion

Inspired by Geertz's definition, George A. Lindbeck, in his suggestive book *The Nature of Doctrine,* describes religion in the following way: "Religions are seen as comprehensive interpretive schemes, usually embodied in myths or narratives and heavily ritualized, which structure human experience and understanding of self and world."[4] Central to religion's function is the question of meaning, of ultimate meaning, and the greatest threat to religion is that of meaninglessness. For as Paul Tillich affirmed in so many different ways, the basic question is: "How do I find meaning in a meaninglessness world?"[5]

It is therefore not accidental that the common address to suffering has been religious. All religious traditions have attempted in various ways to come to grips with the fact of suffering, and most religious traditions are rooted in the belief and the fundamental trust that life is good and meaningful despite the suffering it entails. Religion must constantly ask: Does life have some central meaning despite the suffering and the succession of frustrations and tragedies it brings? For Clifford Geertz, the condition of suffering is "an experiential challenge in whose face the meaningfulness of a particular pattern of life threatens to dissolve into a chaos of thingless names and nameless things."[6] The author then affirms:

> As a religious problem, the problem of suffering is, paradoxically, not how to avoid suffering but how to suffer, how to make of physical pain, personal loss, worldly defeat, or the helpless contemplation of others' agony

something bearable, supportable—something, as we say, sufferable.[7]

It is exactly on this very point that Freud concentrated his attack on religious belief. In Freud's perception, religion is but an illusion because it refuses to accept that life is a struggle that simply ends in the complete defeat of death. For Freud, religion is a construing of reality that does not accept that the forces of our cosmos are impersonal and hostile.

All revealed religions now known are concerned with the agonizing questions that humankind confronts in the encounter with suffering and death: Does life have a meaning? Is wholeness possible? Why suffering? Each religion offers a vision of reality where such questions are answered. Such a vision is given in narratives and rituals. At the heart of these various religions a rich complex of symbols, stories, and rituals are found which attempt to interpret and illuminate experiences of loss and suffering. Such narratives and symbols have a unique educative power and appeal to the whole person. Symbols and narratives are offered by revealed religions to help humankind identify suffering, name it, and overcome it. Religious narratives and symbols create a world of habitation where persons can somehow feel at home. Such narratives enable the human community to live amid cosmic, social, and historical tensions, and, as such, they have life-affirming qualities.

Christianity and Suffering

Christianity as a religious tradition does not argue against suffering, nor does it proffer a solution; it tells a story about Jesus, the crucified and risen Lord. Christians from the very beginning have claimed that the life, ministry, death, and resurrection of Jesus have made a radical difference for humanity. The paschal mystery as a complex of symbols is Christianity's fundamental response to humanity's ongoing situation of suffering, evil, and death. The paschal mystery emerges out of a series of particular and historical events; as a complex of symbols, the paschal mystery is the symbolic expression of the experiences of a particular historical community. As a complex of symbols, the paschal mystery becomes for the Christian an interpretative framework. When one is experiencing suffering or hostility, recalling the symbolic events of Jesus' life, death, and resurrection becomes the means of comfort and understanding. Paul in his writings asserts that his own apostolic career is homologous with the pattern of the paschal mystery. Central to the paschal mystery and open to diverse interpretation is the affirmation that suffering is redemptive. In his apostolic letter "The Christian Meaning of Human Suffering," Pope John Paul II affirms within the context of the paschal mystery that suffering has mystical and positive significance. "Suffering has a special value in the eyes of the church. It is something good before which the church bows down in reverence with all the depth of her faith in the redemption."[8]

Martin Luther King, Jr. saw as the responsibility of his followers to accept suffering as a way of transforming the situation of oppression.

> Suffering can be a most creative and powerful social force.... The nonviolent say that suffering becomes a powerful social force when you willingly accept that violence on yourself, so that self-suffering stands at the center of the nonviolent movement, and the individuals involved are able to suffer in a creative manner, feeling that unearned suffering is redemptive, and that suffering may serve to transform the social situation.[9]

The paschal mystery is a complex of symbols and stories; in Christianity, it illuminates and interprets the mysterious dimensions of suffering. As such, the paschal mystery appeals to the whole person.

Suffering and the Problem of Theodicy

While religious tradition, of necessity, must address the questions of suffering and death, it is these two realities that are the most problematic for believers. For almost every person of religious conviction, the most difficult test of faith comes with the suffering and death of a loved one. Suffering for the believer always leads to the theodicy problem: If God is all-powerful and all-loving, how can God permit suffering? The basic issue of theodicy is how to put together the fact of suffering and belief in the existence of a loving and all-powerful God. The theodicy question originates in two felt needs: a sense that the human situation is much worse off for any reasonable explanation, and the ongoing need for fundamental trust. The theodicy aspect of the experience of suffering simply means that for believers the question of suffering must be approached in the light of the fundamental insights of a religious tradition. Yet there is a basic consensus today that no complete or satisfactory answer can be found to the question of suffering and evil in religious traditions. Edward Schillebeeckx writes: "Evil and suffering are the dark stain upon our history to which no one can offer a solution and which we cannot reconcile with a theodicy or ever wipe away with a social critique and the praxis resulting from it (however necessary they may be)."[10] Stanley Hauerwas, emphasizing the meaninglessness of children's suffering, is led to affirm the following: "We have no theodicy that can soften the pain of our death and the death of our children, but we share a common story which makes it possible for us to be with one another especially as we die." And the author continues, "There can be no way to remove the loneliness of the death of leukemic children unless they see witnessed in the lives of those who care for them a confidence rooted in the friendship with God and with one another—that, finally, is the only response we have to 'the problem' of the death of children."[11]

The experience of suffering tends to change one's perception of God; the experience of suffering becomes a critical question about God. This is true of C.S. Lewis, a well-known literary scholar and one of the twentieth century's best known popular writers on Christian theology. In a brief narrative, *A Grief Observed* (1961), C.S. Lewis described his personal experiences during the months following his wife's death. As a deeply religious man, Lewis was seeking comfort from God but, instead of experiencing a consoling presence, he felt that a door was being slammed in his face. This experience transformed his previous understanding of God. "Not that I am (I think) in much danger of ceasing to believe in God. The real danger is of coming to believe such dreadful things about him. The conclusion I dread is not, 'So there's no God after all,' but, 'So this is what God's really like. Deceive yourself no longer.' "[12]

The same kind of theological transformation seems to have taken place for Rabbi Kushner. In his popular book, *When Bad Things Happen to Good People*, Kushner is obliged to let go of cherished beliefs about God.

> I am fundamentally a religious man who has been hurt by
> life, and I wanted to write a book that could be given to the
> person who has been hurt by life—by death, by illness or
> injury, by rejection or disappointment—and who knows in
> his heart that if there is justice in the world, he deserved
> better.
>
> I would write it for all those people who wanted to go on
> believing, but whose anger at God made it hard for them to
> hold on to their faith and be comforted by religion.[13]

For the believer the experience of suffering leads to a critical question
about God.[14]

Theology and Suffering

Yet the struggle with the theodicy question has deepened the
fundamental insights of most religious traditions and the faith of the
believers, and has led theology to a new understanding of God and
man and woman. Theology can be defined initially as reflection on the
meaning and truth of a religious tradition from within a specific cultural situation. The theologian, of necessity, must analyze the symbols of
his religious community in order to discover the specific meaning
inherent to these symbols. Meanings are expressed symbolically and
live in historical communities of interpretation.

The basic contemporary method in theology is that of correlation. Most contemporary theology is devoted to shaping Christian
practice and teachings in dialogue with modern philosophies, culture,
and social practices. Mediating theologians, as they are called, argue
that Christian faith and modernity can and should live together in harmony. The method of correlation in theology is an attempt to harmo-
nize the past tradition and the present situation.

What is being correlated in the Christian tradition is the paschal
mystery and present-day human experience. So Christian theology
seeks to explain the meaning of the complex of symbols that make up
the paschal mystery and its truth to any given age, which involves the
demonstration of its universal relevance. The similarities of fundamental human experiences to those described in the paschal mystery are an

important basis for the possibility of discovering in the Christian story insights for our own situation. The world of experience described in the paschal mystery is made to resonate with the condition of our human experience.[15]

For many contemporary theologians, theology is perceived as an understanding of the paschal mystery in terms of the experience of suffering. It is their contention that the fundamental question today as in the past is that of suffering. The implication of this statement is that the basic human experience is that of finiteness, of negativity, of contrast. Walter Kasper writes: "No one has experienced humanity to the full unless he or she has experienced its finiteness and suffering. But then experience becomes a way of leading into an open immensity, into a mystery that is ever greater and never to be completely plumbed."[16] The question of suffering forces upon us the most serious questions about the meaning and goal of human life. Every epoch has its own answer to the question of suffering, but the inadequacy of each answer inevitably leads every new generation to pursue the search.

It is not surprising then that Gustavo Gutierrez, in his book *On Job: God-Talk and the Suffering of the Innocent,* affirms that the basic task of theology today is: "How are we to speak of the God of life when cruel murder on a massive scale goes on in the 'corner of the dead'?"[17] Dorothy Soelle has written concerning feminist theology that all true theology begins in suffering. "Theology originates in our need for more, in our sense of failure, in our awareness of life destroyed. Its locus is suffering or the disregard for life that we experience all the time."[18] Carter Heyward seems to affirm the same understanding. "The experience of suffering—actual endurance of pain—is foundational to an authentic understanding of the need for redemption. It is not that we should "seek suffering" as a spiritual path. Rather, we cannot avoid it if we are living fully human, passionate lives in solidarity with one another and other creatures."[19] According to Walter Kasper:

> Insights into the suffering that is inherent in human exis-
> tence have changed the situation of theology. Whereas
> modern theology's partner in dialogue used to be the
> enlightened unbeliever, the partner in dialogue of any con-
> temporary theology is suffering man who has concrete
> experience of the persisting situation of disaster and is

therefore conscious of the weakness and finiteness of his
human existence.[20]

Since suffering is an existential of the human reality, "a theology
that takes the human experience of suffering as its starting point starts,
therefore, not with a borderline phenomenon but with the center and
depths of human existence."[21]

A title of a book by Arthur McGill makes an important point:
Suffering: A Test of Theological Method. Suffering poses the fundamental test for theology in different ways. Primarily it is a test for theology, because theology has to do with God-in-relation, God-for-us.
The most significant question in theology has to do with the difference
God makes for us. So the question of suffering and the question of God
cannot be separated.

Suffering and Salvation

Within the situation of suffering, the major theological question
becomes one about salvation; the question of salvation becomes the
point of departure for the God-question. As Kasper writes: "The concern is therefore always with the concrete God who is the salvation of
human beings and whose glory is man alive."[22] Writing about religion
in general, Raymond Panikkar can affirm:

> In spite of the scores of attempts at defining religion I may
> venture this simple and brief statement. Religion is the
> path Man follows in order to reach the purpose of life, or,
> shorter, religion is the *way of salvation.* One has to add
> immediately that here the words "way" and "salvation" do
> not claim any specific content; rather they stand for the
> existential pilgrimage Man undertakes in the belief that
> this enterprise will help him achieve the final purpose or
> end of life.[23]

So the question of salvation is a human constant since suffering is universal. Religious questions usually have to do with the nature of salvation; religions are fundamentally soteriological.

The salvific path proposed by Christianity is that of the paschal mystery. It is that specific complex of symbols that has provided the Christian community with meaning and significance. The paschal mystery has provided sources of meaning in terms of which all of human existence has been given its basic order and significance.

Suffering and the Cultural Context

Christian theology as Christian must be understood as a critical, reflective and systematic effort to understand the paschal mystery.[24] The basic logic of Christian theology is one of participatory interest of engagement and solidarity. At the same time that Christian theology is existential, it is necessarily hermeneutical. The paschal mystery as the foundational complex of symbols has been interpreted in various ways in the past and is in need of interpretation today. The existential situation of every theologian is always one that is in movement. Such movement carries with it changes of meaning and therefore the necessity of reinterpretation. Various factors influence the actual interpretation of the paschal mystery. The possibility of nuclear war is clearly one of these factors. According to Sallie McFague, "I see the threat of a nuclear holocaust as epitomizing the genuinely novel context in which all constructive work in our time, including theology, must take place."[25] The historical fact of the Jewish holocaust is also a challenge to any interpretation of the paschal mystery. According to J.B. Metz, we must beware of any theological statement made after the holocaust that is unchanged from how it was previously expressed.[26]

The holocaust presents a crisis of faith, the occasion of a "hermeneutical rupture." As David Tracy writes in his introduction to Arthur Cohen's *The Tremendum: A Theological Interpretation of the Holocaust:* "To think the Holocaust is the *tremendum* of the overwhelming power of a radical evil that suspends thought and action alike is to force theologians to think again."[27] For Tracy, serious theological thought is necessitated by the event of the holocaust; the holocaust becomes a test for thoughtful theology.

While both of these factors influence any interpretation of the paschal mystery, the contemporary cultural context also plays a significant role. Interpreting the paschal mystery toward a theology of suffering can only occur concretely within the forms of a particular culture.

Our contemporary culture is characterized by its overwhelming attempt
to eliminate negativity; it is marked by the repression of pain and the
consequent incapacity to suffer; it fosters the incapacity to confront
and appropriate the reality of suffering.

Such an incapacity has been named psychic numbing by Robert
Lifton. The contemporary cultural images, social norms, and models
for and of humanhood are not conducive to the facing of suffering.
According to Robert Lifton and Eric Olson, "The whole age in which
we live is one of vast numbing and desensitization...."[28] Every culture
has its own specific pathology; ours has been described as narcissism.
The narcissistic personality is characterized by its inability to recognize how others feel; pathological narcissists suffer from apathy.[29]

Contemporary theologians in every area of theology—in scripture, ethics, and systematic theology—have perceived suffering as the
starting question for theology. While they may belong to diverse
schools of thought, they have in common their concern for suffering.
This book is about such theologians.

1
A Biblical View of Suffering: Walter Brueggemann

Introduction

Every Christian theology must go by way of the scriptures, and this is especially true of a theology that centers itself on the situation of suffering. Christian theology has fundamentally to do with the articulation of the biblical vision. According to Colin Gunton, "Systematic theology is any activity in which some attempt is made to articulate the Christian gospel or aspects of it with due respect to such dimensions as coherence, universality, and truth."[1] For theology to be Christian, it must be informed by scripture. As Gunton affirms, "Scripture, as the book of God, is the way by which God makes possible that community of worship and life, one of whose activities is systematic theology."[2] Although contemporary theology views itself primarily as reflection upon the actual faith experience of the theologian, it is also hermeneutical and therefore deeply engaged with and challenged by the text. A contemporary theology of suffering cannot ignore the place and role of suffering in the biblical sources. So we begin our investigation with a biblical scholar, Walter Brueggemann.

Walter Brueggemann is a biblical scholar who agrees that all true theology begins in pain. "It is the reality of concrete pain known in the specificity of a person or a community which is the locus of serious faith."[3] His contribution to the theology of suffering lies in his awareness of current trends in Old Testament scholarship and other major fields of learning. His grasp of the new dimensions of biblical scholarship such as sociological and literary analysis makes his work in the area of suffering of significant importance. He has in various ways and at different times addressed the basic question of biblical theology. While recognizing the complexity of issues surrounding biblical theology and the lack of consensus on either its task or its method, Brueggemann has proposed some very suggestive approaches concerning the fundamental organizational principles for a biblical theology.

According to Brueggemann, historical criticism, when perceived as the unique approach to a text, "has become a mode of silencing the text by eliminating its artistic, dramatic and subversive power."[4] Historical criticism has a tendency "to explain away from the text all the hurts and hopes that do not conform to that ideology of objectivity."[5] For Walter Brueggemann, the Old Testament mediates theological reflection through disclosures of hurt and articulation of hope: "I suggest that hurt and hope are the most characteristic aspects of Jewish experience and discourse."[6]

Scripture and Revelation

Brueggemann's criticism of the historical critical method begins with a basic affirmation of the revelatory nature of the scriptures. "The conviction that scripture is revelatory literature is a constant, abiding conviction among the communities of Jews and Christians which gather around the book."[7] But how is the scripture revelatory? In agreement with Jürgen Habermas' understanding that all knowledge is contextual, and connected to special interests, Brueggemann affirms the following:

> The revelatory power of the text is discerned and given precisely through the action of interpretation which is always concrete, never universal, always contextualized, never "above the fray," always filtered through vested interest, never in disinterested purity.[8]

What is true of the process of reception of a revelatory text is also true of the writing of the text.

> That is, not only in its hearing, but also in its speaking, the
> text makes its disclosure in ways that are concrete, contex-
> tualized, and filtered through vested interest.[9]

In emphasizing the contextuality of all texts, the historical-criti-
cal method has clearly indicated that the interpretive act is not really
objective, forcing us to realize that "we are not only meaning receivers
but we are also meaning makers. We not only accept meanings offered
but we construct meanings which we advocate."[10] The implication of
such a realization is that revelation as affirmer of the scriptures is not
simply a process of a once-and-for-all disclosure "but is an ongoing act
of disclosing which will never let the disclosure be closed."[11]
Revelation as disclosure is a historical process involving the interaction of choices and situations. Revelation and interpretation are intimately connected.

This concept of revelation as interpretation is related to the emergence of two methods of scriptural exegesis—the sociological analysis
and the literary analysis. The sociological approach forces us "to ask
about the social intention and social function of a text in relation to the
community and the situation upon which the text impinges."[12] Texts
both in their inception and in their reception cannot be disconnected
from the social processes that mark the community that generates or
interprets them.

Literary analysis on the other hand emphasizes the imaginative
construing of a world by the text.[13] The world revealed in the scriptural
texts could not be disclosed apart from the text. To choose between
different texts is to choose between different worlds.

> Literary analysis assumes that the text is not a one-dimen-
> sional statement, but is an offer of a world that has an inte-
> riority, in which the text is not a monolithic voice, but is a
> conversation out of which comes a new world.[14]

Looking at scripture as revelatory from the perspectives of these
two different methods, it becomes clear that scripture as revelation is
not a flat, obvious offer of a conclusion, but it is an ongoing conversa-
tion which evokes, invites and offers. It is the process of the text itself,
in which each interpretive generation participates, that is the truth of

revelation.[15] It is within this very complex process that God's ever new word and new truth are mediated to each new generation.

Scripture and Religious Language

These two methods indicate that religious language emerges not simply as a response to revelation but also as constitutive of the disclosive nature of the texts. The religious worlds of the biblical texts are not simply given for inhabitation, but they are also construed. According to Brueggemann, such religious worlds are "chosen, guarded, justified, defended, maintained at least partly with intentionality."[16] Such worlds present in and presented by the texts did not exist before they were articulated, so that "speech leads reality and until reality is spoken we did not know reality, perceive it or embrace it.... Imaginative speech not only describes, but constitutes reality."[17] For Brueggemann, these two methods have made clear that the creator God's self-revelation is ever active in our midst and that that activity reveals to us a world that is open-ended. Being created to the image of God implies for Brueggemann that we share "in God's imaging activity."[18]

Theology as a Constitutive Act

What is true of scripture as a revelatory enterprise is also true of theology. Following Gordon Kaufmann, our author perceives theology as "a constitutive act, in which our discernment of God must be reconstituted in wholly new ways."[19] Such a reconstitution is "constructive in some sense for the faith of the Church."[20] God in himself remains always incomprehensible even in light of our claims about the revelatory power of the scriptures. What is available about God is our imaginative construct of God. "Even for one who accepts the particularity of Jesus as the clue to the real referent, the practical truth is that, even in our discernment of Jesus, we are dealing in important ways with imaginative reconstructions."[21]

So in the various forms of biblical exegesis, Brueggeman sees the convergence of modes of speech, religious claims and social settings. While the scriptures are truly faith documents and make available to all generations a message of faith, they are also theologies. These theologies are not handed down to us on a platter ready for consumption. Neither theology nor message can simply be reduced to simple statements or monolithic creeds. Both message and theology are in the process of becoming. For Brueggemann, "It has become increasingly clear that reality is not fixed and settled, that it cannot be described objectively."[22] As personal agent we are not simply encountered by objective reality but we also have been given the capacity to constitute the world. So not only do we describe what lies out there but we also evoke what is not yet realized. The theologian has the capacity of bringing about new worlds through speech. "Responsible theology must be a constitutive act, in which our discernment of God must be reconstituted in wholly new ways."[23] The theologian finds himself or herself on a restless journey and must commend a "trusted memory" and "a faithful voice."[24]

Bi-Polar Structure of Scripture

The "trusted memory" and the "faithful voice" of the theologian must concern themselves with the fundamental trajectories of the biblical tradition. Brueggemann identifies the basic characteristics of these trajectories in terms of "royal" and "liberation." The royal trajectory is universalistic in intention, socially conservative, and emphasizes God's glory and holiness, and that of institutions fostering such holiness. The "liberation trajectory" is more concrete and historically minded in perspective, socially revolutionary and transformative, and focuses on God's justice and righteousness. Following this bi-polar structure of the scriptures, the theologian's faith itself must be understood in a bi-polar mode.

Since faith is bi-polar, theology will also itself be bi-polar. This bi-polarity serves "to legitimate structure and to embrace pain."[25] The theology of the Old Testament embraces both a "common" theology that legitimates existing structures and a more "radical" theology that embraces the pain of the conflictual social process. An understanding of God emerges in the ambiguity of the experience of pain.

Common Theology and Liberation Theology

The Old Testament is characterized by two different modes of theology: a "common" theology and a "liberation" theology. The "common" theology centers on a monarchical understanding of God and emphasizes God's sovereignty and providence. It legitimates those who are in power and offers a basic theodicy for those who experience suffering. While such a theology is prevalent in the ancient Near East, this theology does not fully express Israel's faith experience. From within the covenantal relationship with God, Israel senses that its God is not only an "enforcer" and a legitimator of existing structures, but one who also embraces Israel's pain. A specific understanding of God emerges in the ambiguity of the experience of pain. There is a bi-polar nature to Israel's God: God emerging in the social process and God standing beyond historical contingencies.[26] The God who embraces pain is a God who no longer follows society's ways; it is a God who "has broken with the usual notions of retribution."[27] God's holiness "is re-characterized as compassion."[28] By embracing pain, God's own self is transformed. "God's heart is impinged upon.... God is not able to do the warranted act, precisely because God is no longer able to be a one-dimensional legitimator of structure. Now God is transformed by the embrace of pain in God's own person, which changes the calculus with reference to Israel."[29] What is true of God is also true of us. "Human personhood in the image of this God always entails pain-embrace which causes transformation and breaks beyond contractual relationships."[30] The critical and criticizing element for Israel's theology is pain. The key element is always pain.[31]

Faith and Suffering

For Brueggemann, the fundamental aspect of Israel's faith has to do with pain. "I suggest that this question of pain, experienced as personal hurt, as expressed in the lament Psalms or in the public outcry which leads to liberation (cf. Exod. 2:23-25), is the main question of Old Testament faith."[32] This is not simply true for Israel's faith, but also for our faith.

As Brueggemann writes: "What we make of pain is perhaps the most telling factor for the question of life and the nature of our faith."[33]

Here it is not simply a question of how one deals with suffering, but also with "social valuing of the pained and the pain-bearers, the poor, the useless, the sick, and the other marginal ones."[34]

Brueggemann's basic approach to the scriptures is parabolic; the Old Testament is odd and disruptive. It embodies the discourses that shaped Israel as a distinctive community. It is characterized by its articulation of "disclosures of hurt and of hope."[35] The human experiences of hurt and hope provide the basic element for Israel's discourse about God.[36]

The emergence of Israel's faith lies in an experience of disorder that clearly impedes the development of human experience. While that disorder has cosmic dimensions and natural causes, its clearest reason is the "historical disorder arising out of unjust, exploitative, oppressive arrangements of social power and social goods."[37] For Brueggemann, the exodus event is a paradigmatic expression of this disorder and not primarily one about God's powerful deliverance. "In fact it is the hurt of Israel that is the driving reality of the Exodus tradition."[38] The hurtful disorder as acknowledged is "a fundamental act of courage and of subversion."[39] In Israel hurt/suffering is not only experienced, but it is noticed; it is not only noticed, but it is also voiced. Such voicing "is a bold act of self-assertion and political subversion."[40] The voiced hurt is also heard in heaven by none other than Yahweh. God, according to Brueggemann, "is bonded to Israel around the quintessential human reality of hurt."[41] In fact the linkage of God to God's creation is through a voiced and noticed hurt. God's hearing is not simply a passive act, but it is expressive of God's solidarity with the one hurting. Such a noticing and voicing of hurt have implications for public life and policy. "Israel's public power and its institutional forms must be ordered to eliminate the cause of such voiced hurt."[42] The experience of hurt shapes the basic ethical structures in Israel's existence. It brings about specific models of social relationship, and the Jubilee Year a time of release from debt and bondage.

Suffering and Hope

While hurt must be voiced and noticed, this is accompanied by the anticipation of its resolution. "Israel's hope is that there will be a decisive and radical reordering of social power and social goods, so that all may have enough, none will have too much, and all will live together in harmony."[43] While that act of expectation is clearly a theological one, it "is also a profound, elemental material yearning rooted in the very bodies of the hurting ones, a yearning that moves with authority from hurting bodies to hoping lips."[44] While hope is in God, its origin is in bodily hurt; for when such hurt is noticed, it is noticed as unacceptable.

The liturgy of Israel also expresses noticed and voiced hurt, and it is this liturgy which "socializes its young and initiates them into this mode of experience, speech, social perception, and public practice."[45] The liturgy functions as a model for social relations, for "without the liturgy the next generation might let the hurt go unnoticed and unvoiced, might let the world become settled, might reckon social hurt to be a normal, acceptable cost for social tranquility."[46] The liturgy consistently invites critical refusal to passively accepted hurt and invites active resistance.

The Language of the Laments

Liturgy has a rehabilitative and restorative function. This is especially true of Israel's liturgical prayers which serve "both to *enable* the experience so that dimensions of it are not lost and to *limit* the experience so that dimensions are denied their legitimacy."[47] So those who suffer can protest their experience in a legitimate life-world. The liturgy is a powerful medium to bring hurt to words and to articulation, and "bringing hurt to public expression is an important first step in the dismantling criticism that permits a new reality, theological and social, to emerge."[48] This is especially true of Israel's liturgical prayers, the laments. The form of the lament is dialogical and implies a covenantal relation to God. "The lament witnesses to a robust form of faith which affirms that God seriously honors his part of the exchange."[49] In the lament, the speaker does expect some action from God, some form of intervention because of covenantal promises. The power of the lament lies in the movement from petition to praise, from alienation to trust.[50] The laments clearly point out that the embrace of pain and its submission to God is the only way that pain can be resolved.

The laments are far from being acts of resignation; they are truly acts of protest and, as such, are better classified as complaints instead of laments. The laments are refusals to accept reality as it presents itself. Underlying these prayers there is the ongoing hope in the transformative power of God.[51] The God of the laments is clearly not the wholly other God, unapproachable and distant. God is the compassionate God who can come to the aid of those who suffer.

It is interesting to notice that, for Brueggemann, the shape and dynamics of the Psalms can be most usefully understood according to the theological framework of crucifixion and resurrection. Much of the Psalms have the form of complaint and lament. The laments offer an alternative identity; it lets us be open to pain (crucifixion) but also healing and newness (resurrection). "The Crucifixion of Jesus, like the pathos of God himself in the Old Testament, provides a model for all hurtful solidarity which may be practiced with the poor and the powerless."[52] The paschal mystery offers us a Christian way into the basic structure of biblical theology: that of orientation-disorientation-new orientation. "The lament psalm is a painful, anguished articulation of a move into disarray and dislocation."[53] Yet there is always a move from a context of disorientation to a new orientation. "The second move also characterizes many of the Psalms, in the form of songs of thanksgiving and declarative hymns that tell a tale of a decisive time, an inversion, a reversal of fortune, a rescue, deliverance, saving, liberating, healing."[54]

The bi-polar structure of the scriptures and the consequent bi-polar nature of biblical faith set up the framework for the basic theodicy question. For Brueggemann, the struggle of the oppressed against injustice is really the fundamental issue of theodicy. While the quest for communion with God is pervasive in the biblical material, nevertheless, such communion can never be indifferent to the situation of the community. The quest for God is never unrelated to the question of justice, and therefore to the question of theodicy. "Theodicy is concern for a fair deal."[55]

For Brueggemann the question of theodicy is not simply a theological question: it is a question with much social implication. "Serious theodicy is always linked to social arrangements of access and benefit."[56] So the basic theodicy problem, whenever it presents itself, "must be understood sociologically as a question about law, about the rule of law, about the reliability of the system of rewards and punishments. Theodicy . . . concerns the character of God as practiced in the system of values in a social matrix."[57] In considering the Psalms, it becomes apparent that while theodicy always involves a specific understanding of God, it also has much to do with "the rationale or legitimacy for the way in which society is ordered."[58] Theodicy has to do with basic questions about power and powerlessness. "The practical effect is that theodicy is a theory of power about who makes decisions and who obeys them, who administers and controls God, who has access to them and on what terms."[59] Accepted theodicies usually function as forms of social control and every revolution in social structures will lead to a new theodicy. A transformation of society or of an understanding of God is also connected to a change of theodicy.

Suffering and Prophetic Theology

It should now be amply clear that, for Brueggemann, the central focus of the Bible is suffering—the suffering of the people and the suffering of God. And while various forms of theology may take account of suffering, for Brueggemann the most appropriate form should be that of a prophetic theology. The prophets, according to Brueggemann, "were concerned with most elemental changes in most human society and that they understood a great deal about how change is effected. The prophets understood the possibility of change as linked to emotional extremities of life."[60] The basic task of prophecy is to bring about an alternative consciousness. Its basic task "is to hold together criticism and energizing."[61] The criticism is directed to structures that have been absolutized.

The prophets are compassionate people. They share in the suffering of God and of the people. They have a passion about their people's hurt and suffering, and that compassion has its source in their communion with God. Not only did they know God and see reality as God sees it, but they also felt as God felt; they experience God's grief over the suffering of the people. For Brueggemann, "It is the experience of pain which brings discernment about the truth. Those who offer truth without experiencing the pain are likely not to be trusted."[62]

What Brueggemann finds in biblical theology concerning suffering, he also sees as basically necessary for contemporary theology. In biblical writings there is a convergence of social context, literary articulation, and theological claim. "The theological claim is intimately linked to the literary presentation, but both that claim and that articulation are reflective of and in the service of a certain social world."[63] For Brueggemann, faith must be understood as involving an ongoing dialogue with the world. The world to be in dialogue with must be the real world, not one that corresponds to one's ideologies. The first step to authentic faith, and therefore to authentic theology, is a realistic evaluation of the world. The realistic evaluation of reality must take into consideration pain and suffering.

Pain and suffering have different aspects. For Brueggemann, "The most immediate pain consists in relations violated, in intimacy fractured, in alienations, in parents that have lived too long, in children who have stayed too long or left too soon."[64] It is the interpersonal realm, the fact that we are always interdependent, that can bring about so much pain and suffering. Pain can be brought about by situations of unattained goals, by "lives of quiet desperation."[65] There is also a public dimension to pain. Pain emerges when society's expectations are not fulfilled. Many are the victims of society's violence. "Beyond normal informal social outlets, the violence finally turns to policy, to public values and public conduct which foster and legitimate violence."[66] "In a society marked by idolatrous ideologies, doxology, the unrelieved, unreceived, unhonored pain turns to destructive energy, and it is worked against all those who do not 'obey God's laws' and cooperate with the system."[67]

An essential aspect and cause of pain is "relentless hopelessness."[68] Denial and guilt lead to the inability to imagine an alternative vision. "We do not believe there is a God who makes things new, who cares so about truth, equity, and righteousness that the present must give way to the force of God's promise."[69] Within a situation marked by the ever-present possibility of nuclear war, "we cannot imagine a different future for the world, nor for those closest, most precious, most troubled around us."[70] While pain and suffering are clearly part of reality, our grasp of pain and reality is always appropriated culturally. Culture is also part, a very important part, of reality.

Conclusion

Brueggemann's biblical theology addresses itself to a social context perceived as one dominated by "religion without compelling power and . . . a social world that is organized against our own humanity."[71] Our contemporary situation is characterized as numbness. Brueggemann characterizes our society as narcissistic, one supported by consumerism which rests on a value system of satiation and self-indulgence. The religious communities' approach to God is basically a utilitarian one; God is conceived basically as a candy machine in heaven dispensing the longed-for goodies.

The very nature of suffering in its most interpersonal dimension and its cultural context demands a theology based on the prophetic model. This implies that a theology that has no interest in the political and social realm will not be of real importance in the world today. The prophetic theology will be one that will challenge all existing structures to be concerned about the suffering of the people. Such a theology can never be safe and respectable; it can never be simply a question of repeating old answers.

2
God and Suffering: Edward Schillebeeckx

Introduction

To a greater extent than any other contemporary systematic theologian, Edward Schillebeeckx has developed his theology in confrontation with the universal situation of suffering. Indeed, according to this author, "The history of suffering . . . is the constant theme of every account of life, every philosophy, and every religion."[1] Schillebeeckx's concern with suffering has empirical roots. It expresses his fundamental understanding of the nature of salvation as revealed in Christianity, and it also functions as an essential element of his theological method.

Human history and especially the history of religions call our attention to the fact that suffering is never trivialized. This same history also reveals that suffering, while always problematic, is more so when the person suffering believes in God.

While the various religious traditions such as Hinduism, Buddhism, Judaism, Christianity, and the Moslem faiths differ from each other in their understanding of the problem of human suffering, they all share in common an opposition to suffering. They also reject any form of radical dualism and perceive the God-reality as compassion.[2] Religious traditions have attempted in different ways to identify the causes of suffering. For Schillebeeckx this is an important task because it is intimately connected to the various understandings of sal-

vation offered in a variety of religious traditions. Karl Marx located the
origin of suffering in specific social and economic structures. Judaism
saw the basic cause of suffering in humanity's sinfulness, and
Buddhism in man's/woman's greed. All of these various understandings of the causes of suffering led to different theories about salvation
or ways of eliminating suffering. What is historically evident, according to Schillebeeckx, is that religions tend to take suffering very seriously and perceive its eradication as very difficult. "The religious consciousness in particular provokes a more vigorous protest against
suffering, above all unmerited and helpless suffering, than has ever
been the case with critical rationalism (Marxism excepted)."[3] Among
religions, Christianity especially takes the reality of human suffering
seriously and salvation as infinitely costly.

While suffering must be approached in a critical and rational
way, there are dimensions of suffering, such as the suffering of the
innocent, that defy rational explanation. "There is also the suffering of
our finitude, the abiding suffering of the irrevocable tension between
nature and man/woman, the child born severely handicapped, the loneliness of many people, the suffering of death, the suffering of guilt."[4]
Suffering is of major concern for Schillebeeckx. It lies at the center of
his theological method and guides his approach to the interpretation of
the gospel message for our contemporary period. Suffering is especially crucial in christology.

Suffering and Christology

Schillebeeckx's basic question in his christological writings may
be summarized in Jesus' own words: "Who do you say that I am?" For
Schillebeeckx this question can be translated in a more anthropologi-
cal/ethical form: Can we live humanly before God? Here the question
has to do with meaning and meaningfulness which are fundamental to
our cultural situation. Schillebeeckx calls the problem of meaninglessness the "basic human question." Schillebeeckx's focus on meaninglessness and the suffering it engenders accounts for his emphasis of the
experience of failure and especially that of Jesus' on the cross.

According to Schillebeeckx, the critical reappropriation of the
early church's experience handed down to us as message is perhaps
one of the most difficult tasks confronting contemporary christology.

What are those elements of the past that are of contemporary relevance and vitality? What is the authority of the past over the present, or of the present over the past? For Schillebeeckx, the answer lies in his understanding of the nature and role of experience in human existence which also influences his understanding of revelation and faith. This in turn determines Schillebeeckx's understanding of christology.

The Function of Experience

According to Schillebeeckx, human beings learn through experience. The word "experience" is not to be identified simply with subjectivity or emotions. Experience is that which happens when a human subject encounters given reality. In such an encounter both subjectivity and objectivity are connected. Such human encounters are characterized by reflective and cognitive dimensions. Experience then means learning through direct contact with people and things. Yet there is no such thing as a raw experience. Experiences occur within an acquired framework which makes understanding possible. New perceptions on our part are possible only if somehow connected to previous experiences. In some fashion one can say that the more experienced one is, the more open one is to other experiences. There is a cumulative and qualitative dimension to our experiencing.

In a sense experience is always for us experience "as," that is, experience with interpretation. The experience of ourselves and the world cannot be completely analyzed in terms of the difference between objective and subjective. For example, to find salvation in Jesus is not either a subjective experience or an objective fact. The experience of salvation is the experience of an objective reality and an interpretation at the same time.

While there is a large dimension of continuity in our understanding of reality and a real dependence on tradition, there is also a place for novelty. Reality as experienced is always placed within an already given framework. At times reality resists our frameworks and forces us to new understanding. New encounters with reality, new experiences can be critical of past interpretations and productive of new understanding. Schillebeeckx suggests that within this framework of understanding, new experiences can claim real authority while failing to confirm past understanding. "Truth comes near to us by the alienation

and disorientation of what we have already achieved and planned."[5]
Reality in many instances is refractory and resists our attempts to control it. "People learn from failures—where their projects are blocked
and they make a new attempt, in sensitive reverence for the resistance
and thus for the orientation of reality."[6] Because of the "givenness"
nature of reality, reality is often perceived by the subject as coming
from beyond and as such appears to be disclosive and revelatory. It is
often the finite nature of reality, its aspect of "limit" or "boundary" that
leads to the fundamental question of the meaning of human existence.
Here the hermeneutical principle for the disclosure of reality is not the
self-evidence but the scandal, the stumbling block of the refractoriness
of reality. Schillebeeckx posits the experience of creatureliness as the
foundation of all religious awareness. By this Schillebeeckx means "an
experience of ourselves, others and the world in which we feel as a
norm something which transcends at least our arbitrary control of ourselves."[7]

Experience and Revelation

For Schillebeeckx, the revelation of God in the human context is
always indirect and dialectical. Human experiences are not equally disclosive of God; some experiences bring about a "breakthrough" in our
ordinary existence that makes us question the meaningfulness of existence and can lead to personal conversion. Certain experiences, some
positive and others negative, are "limit" or "boundary" experiences
that push us beyond the immediacy of our existence toward a reality
that transcends us, a reality of deeper dimension. Suffering and the
threat of death as experiences of meaninglessness within the ongoing
search for meaning are such experiences. They are disclosures of a
possible future quite radically different than the present. Such experiences are for Schillebeeckx "contrast experience." For as individuals
react to evil and suffering not with despair, but with hope, then is disclosed an extra dimension that sustains humanity. Such experiences are
the very ground of any claim that at the core of reality there lies a mystery of compassion. Such contrast experiences are revelatory but in a
dialectical and indirect way. Revelation for Schillebeeckx can be
understood as "the crossing of a boundary within the dimension of

human existence."[8] What is formal to revelation is that it is the crossing of a boundary.

Revelation of God in Jesus Christ will be understood by Schillebeeckx as the crossing of a boundary. As disclosure of God, revelation always happens as experience, for all encounters with the divine are mediated through creatures. So revelation of God must be understood as encounter. For Schillebeeckx, encounter is the most pervasive and fundamental mode of existence, of embodied existence, and embodied consciousness. Encounter then becomes the ground of any interpersonal relation to others and to God. Revelation as encounter with God is always a mediated experience, the experience being one of contrast; as revelatory it opens up a new and genuine future that comes from God's compassionate and creative power.

Religious faith is the experience of reality as having its ground in transcendent compassion. Such a faith always comes to word, and, because of the social and historical nature of the human person, faith occurs in the context of a traditionary process. So God's revelation is "*experienced* by believers and *interpreted* in religious language and therefore expressed in human terms, in the dimension of our utterly human history."[9] The initiative of revelation, as God's offer of self, always lies with God; yet as revelation it occurs in the context of a response, so faith is a fundamental horizon within which reality is perceived and interpreted. Faith language becomes the grammar of God's compassionate presence within creation; this language will by necessity be symbolic, evocative and indirect.

Revelation and Culture

As a traditionary process, religious faith functions as an interpretative framework. The manifestation of God in Jesus Christ claimed by Christianity to be uniquely salvific and of universal value, and experienced by the early church, has become a message handed down in a living tradition. "What was experience for others yesterday is tradition for us today, and what is experience for us today will in turn be tradition for others tomorrow."[10] There are no unmediated or ahistorical encounters with Jesus Christ. No formulation of any encounter with Jesus is possible without some specific cultural expressions. While the message of the gospel intends to be "transcultural," yet it has come to

expression in the form of particular cultures. "Only in the concrete and
in the particular can the Gospel be the revelation of the universality of
God and his salvation."[11] As Schillebeeckx writes again: "Cultural
forms are constitutive mediations of the explicit message of revelation.
God's revelation in Jesus is an event independent of men and women
and their experiences and history; but it is experienced and put into
words in the form of a religious tradition of accumulative experiences
and interpretations by human beings."[12]

In any encounter with Jesus Christ there must be two poles: the
cultural forms of the past and the present-day cultural forms. An
encounter with Jesus Christ involves " 'the encounter of cultures,' a
'culture shock,' or confrontation of cultures that draw their vitality
from the Christian Gospel and acclimatize it in their own cultural
forms."[13] The basic point in question becomes that of the historical
identity, one of particularity and universality, of that which is permanent in the message and what is transitory, or what is normative and
what is relative. For Schillebeeckx the question of identity can only be
found "on the level of the corresponding relation between the original
message (tradition) and the always different situation, both in the past
and in the present."[14] It is not a question of the terms, of message and
situation, but of the relations between those terms. "The relation of
equality between these relations carries within itself the Christian identity of meaning."[15] The unity and identity is one of depth. "It is a process of an always new 'cultural incorporation' of the Gospel's transcultural substance of faith, which itself can never be found or received
outside a particular cultural form."[16]

Theology and Praxis

So the process of interpretation becomes a "creative process of
giving meaning, a re-reading of the tradition from within a new situation."[17] Theology therefore cannot simply be reduced to "a theoretical
interpretation of the Christian past";[18] praxis, i.e. the actual living faith,
is essential to theology itself. "Christianity is not a message which has
to be believed, but an experience of faith which becomes a message,
and as an explicit message seeks to offer a new possibility of life experience to others who hear it from within their own experience."[19] So it
is a question of living the truths, and the Christian tradition can be

handed down through a living history of discipleship. The basic claim that at the core of all reality lies a compassionate God can only be somehow warranted in discipleship. So the Christian tradition has to be one not only of meaning but also of liberation.

> The Christian faith's tradition of experience and interpretation is a tradition of *meaning* with *liberating force.* It opens a horizon of possible experience for us today also. What we are dealing with here is not primarily a theoretical disclosure of meaning, but first and foremost a *narrative* revelation of meaning, which nevertheless was already being accompanied by at least an initial theological reflection even in the Old and New Testament.[20]

Authentic discipleship which by necessity must be a liberating one will bring about new traditions, new narratives. Thus "every community throughout the world has to write its own history of the living Jesus.... The account of the life of Christians in the world in which they live is a fifth gospel; it also belongs at the heart of Christology."[21]

Christology and Suffering

Every christology is an ongoing attempt to thematize the universal significance of the particular event that Jesus is. Every "christology" implies a process of mediation, i.e. finding an intermediary factor between the historical Jesus and his universal significance. That mediating point is, for Schillebeeckx, the history of human suffering. Schillebeeckx focuses upon the universal and historical fact of human suffering and the ongoing human experiences of contrast as the basic mediating points in christology. Such a mediating point cannot simply be theoretical but it is by essence participatory in nature, demanding solidarity with those who in this world suffer.

Suffering for Schillebeeckx emerges as the privileged locus of revelation both of what lies beyond us and of what makes us be who we actually are. The experience of suffering leads to a prophetic stance toward reality, to the ongoing proclamation that "reality ought to be different," to the calling into question reality as it is and how it is justified. "In the prophetic Jesus," according to Schillebeeckx, "mysticism and the healing of men/women came from one and the same source: his experience of the contrast between the living God and the history of human suffering."[22] Jesus' own ministry is characterized by contemplation and emancipatory action aimed at liberation and bringing about human salvation. The basic framework is clearly one of eschatological expectation and anticipation of universal meaningfulness.

Suffering, as Schillebeeckx points out, is a universal fact: all ages and all religions have attempted to come to terms with suffering and yet suffering remains a mystery. "Both philosophy and theology stand bereft of counsel and speech, faced with this complete totality of evil and of human suffering, brought about by nature, by persons and by structures."[23] History as Schillebeeckx perceives it reveals that a world free from suffering is fundamentally a utopian vision.

The Nature of Suffering

Suffering is a complex reality as it is perceived in the history of humanity. Suffering is not always a negative reality although it may be perceived as such. In fact, "A world in which there was no place for suffering and sorrow, even for deep grief, would seem to be inhuman, a world of robots, even an unreal world."[24] Certain suffering when borne with courage and dignity can contribute to the maturity of an individual. There is also the suffering for a good cause, a suffering motivated by sacrificial love. "Suffering is the likely consequence in this world of any whole-hearted sacrifice for a great cause: suffering through and for others."[25] There is also suffering brought about because of the perceived absence and hiddenness of God.

While there can be certain benefits to suffering, there is far too great an "excess" of suffering in the world to ever justify its existence. Always confronting humanity, there is the unmerited suffering, the suffering of the innocent, for which there cannot be any rational or logical explanation. "There is suffering which is not even suffering 'for a good cause,' but suffering in which men/women, without finding meaning for themselves, are simply made the crude victims of an evil cause which serves others."[26] That kind of suffering provokes scandal, a scandal which cannot have "a specific structural place in the divine plan."[27] That kind of scandalous suffering cannot be categorized simply as a problem that cannot simply be solved, because before such suffering human logic stands mute.

For Schillebeeckx, the only meaningful response that can be made to such suffering is to resist it.[28] Evil has no right to exist and such a refusal is "consistent and coherent if it is linked with a powerful involvement in resistance against all forms of evil."[29] Yet there can be no total victory over suffering, no complete resistance, for there is always death. "Death above all shows that we are deluded if we think that we can realize on earth a true, perfect, and universal salvation for all and for every individual."[30]

Suffering and Death

For man's/woman's resistance against evil—laudable as it is—is circumscribed by a very specific reality of experience; in Schillebeeckx's own words, there is "the tension between 'nature' and 'history' which makes up man's/woman's transitory life and can *never be removed,* a dialectic of which death is merely an extreme opponent, the boundary situation."[31] Death brings the "final fiasco" of man's/woman's efforts at resisting evil into stark relief. It shatters our illusions that we can somehow find on earth perfect salvation for all. For if salvation is to be real, total, and complete, it must somehow include the elimination of all suffering and evil—an impossibility for earthly man/woman whose history is ultimately overtaken by his or her "nature," i.e. by death.

Theodicy and the God of Salvation

The real history of suffering confronts us with a theological problem, that of God and suffering, the basic question of theodicy which, within Christianity, becomes a question about salvation. Human history, past, present, and future, poses the basic question of "Whether some salvific activity on God's part does indeed take place in Jesus of Nazareth...."[32] The existence of scandalous suffering becomes a question about God, "the ultimate determining reality," the God of Jesus Christ.

It is Schillebeeckx's ongoing contention that at the core of most religious traditions is the basic understanding that God is essentially a compassionate God. "If God is really God, he is pure positiveness."[33] While Christianity has no solution to the problem of suffering,[34] "Jesus' interpretation of suffering is connected with his deep personal relationship with God."[35] Revealed in that deep relationship is that "God and suffering are diametrically opposed: where God appears, evil and suffering have to yield."[36] So "we cannot look for the ground of suffering in God . . . " for in Schillebeeckx's mind God is pure positivity, the opponent of evil.[37]

God does not want men or women to suffer "but wills to *overcome* suffering where it occurs in our history."[38] "God wants men's/women's salvation and in it victory over their suffering."[39] Now salvation must be expressed "in terms of the integrity of human life."[40] In the same way that suffering cannot be reduced to political or social causes, salvation must entail wholeness. Salvation cannot be separated from human liberation "for salvation from God is always salvation for men/women with all that that implies for truly human life...."[41] So salvation simply "cannot be found outside suffering."[42] "Salvation is wholeness and no man/woman is made whole as long as disaster and oppression, injustice and misery, prevail around him/her."[43]

Salvation, since it is for us, must take place in our world and take human form. That human form is the person of Jesus Christ. ". . . Jesus can be recognized as the manifestation of the universal love of God in the form of a human person...."[44] Jesus' life and message centered on God as Abba, God as boundless love. Such a God cannot require the death of Jesus for our salvation. Human suffering, Jesus' own suffering, cannot be attributed to God. God is present in the suffering and death of Jesus as overcoming suffering itself. In fact, belief in the paschal mystery means basic trust in God's ultimate victory over suffering.

Salvation and Jesus' Suffering

Schillebeeckx's opposition to any negativity in God goes counter to much traditional theology and has consequences for our understanding of suffering, especially as such suffering is perceived as redemptive. As Jesus' death became detached from its historical context (i.e. a suffering through and for others as a consequence of his critical preaching), people began to "theologize" his death. It came to be seen as a necessary ingredient in the drama of a God who, while desiring reconciliation with sinful man, had to defend his honor. Jesus was to suffer and die as penance for the sins of others who could not perform adequate penance themselves; only in this way—that is, by the suffering and death of the "God-Man"—could God's honor be avenged (or satisfied). Suffering became a way of appeasing God—and atoning for one's sins—and thus lost its necessary critical force.

According to Schillebeeckx, "The death of Jesus was no coincidence but the intrinsic historical consequence of the radicalism of both his message and his lifestyle, which showed that all 'master/servant' relationships were incompatible with the Kingdom of God."[45] The death of Jesus is the "historical expression of the unconditional character of his proclamation and practice."[46] Schillebeeckx sees the foundation of Jesus' activity, which ultimately led him to the cross, in his experience of deep intimacy with God. Abba, Jesus' God, is the one opposed to suffering and who refuses evil to have the last word. Jesus' hope is grounded not in his experience of this world and its history of suffering but in his personal experience in a God of life. "Jesus' interpretation of suffering is connected with his deep personal relationship with God, the heart of his life. God and suffering are diametrically opposed: when God appears, evil and suffering have to yield."[47] In his life, ministry and death, Jesus is the parable of God, a parable about God's compassionate care for us.

In the parabolic nature of Jesus' life, ministry, message, and death, Jesus' death is perceived as basically negative, as violence done to Jesus, as a basic human failure, as a "fiasco." The Gethsemane account tells us that Jesus did not fully understand God's way but yet trusted God. So the meaning of Jesus' death cannot be separated from Jesus' life and message. "At precisely this point we see the critical barrenness of theological speculations which neglect the circumstances of Jesus' death and consider that death in and of itself, almost detached from the specific Jesus of Nazareth, then going on to ascribe to that death various world-embracing, universal saving meanings."[48] Jesus did not seek suffering, nor did he seek his death, but because of his radical love he was unconcerned about the consequences for his life.

"This was an intrinsic consequence of his proclamation and lifestyle, which was more important to him than the saving of his life."[49] And again, "Anyone who sets no limits to his sacrifice for the suffering of others will sooner or later have to pay with his life—even today. Jesus came to terms with this."[50]

Love as Redemptive

So what is redemptive is not the negativity of suffering and death but the positivity of love. "Suffering is not redemptive in itself, but it is redemptive when it is suffering through and for others..."[51] Schillebeeckx then goes on to affirm "that only love is redemptive, because it essentially guarantees a person's existence, accepts them, confirms them and endorses them. Love is taking the side of another person."[52] Redemptive love is a love which transforms or forgives. Universal redemption can only be brought about by a universal and perfect love which can only be that of God. Yet human love in its finite and particular dimension can be the visible expression of God's unconditional, universal love. "Supported by this [God's] absolute love, human love becomes the sacrament of God's redemptive love. In fact, ultimately God's love is tested through the action of our 'orthopractic' love."[53] Our own experience of suffering on behalf of others is an authentic imitation of Jesus, "an active *memoria passionis* of the Risen Lord."[54] God's unconditional love lived out in Jesus' own existence and ultimately leading Jesus to the cross is confirmed in the resurrection. The ultimate Christian answer to suffering is that God's love as expressed in the resurrection of Jesus "transcends these negative aspects in our history, not so much by allowing them as by *overcoming them*, making them as though they had not happened."[55]

The resurrection of Jesus, in other words, shows God's determination not to "allow" the negativity of suffering and death, but to overcome them, to "correct" them, to "undo" their disastrous effects. Accordingly, we are not redeemed by Jesus' death—how could an event so shameful and negative be "redeeming" in any sense?—but is redeemed *despite* it, a "despite" that God transcends by his unconditional victory over the negative and destructive aspects of history.

Suffering and Resurrection

The meaning of all of this is that God does not want man/woman to suffer, but wills instead to overcome his/her suffering where it occurs in history. Indeed, the uncompromising message of Jesus is that God's "mystery of mercy" will triumph over the "mystery of unrighteousness"; God will turn to good effect all of the negativity and all of the suffering produced by the "initiative" of finitude. In light of the paschal mystery, suffering and death take on a different meaning. Yet suffering and death still remain impenetrable. Jesus' resurrection is the object of our faith, of our hope. As Schillebeeckx writes: "Our faith in the Resurrection is itself still a prophecy and a promise for this world—qua prophecy unsheltered and unprotected, defenseless and vulnerable. And so the life of the Christian is not visibly 'justified' by the facts of history. . . . The servant is not greater than his Lord. Just as Jesus did, the Christian takes the risk of entrusting himself and the vindication of his living to God; he is prepared to receive the vindication where Jesus did: beyond death."[56]

Schillebeeckx's analysis and understanding of the paschal mystery offer us much on the Christian perception of suffering. In the paschal mystery we are assured that neither suffering nor death can separate us from God and that the basic negativity of suffering will be overcome, an assurance that should lead us to greater freedom and action against innocent suffering and the power of evil. Resurrection makes manifest that the "failure" of suffering and death has been "overturned," and that our basic concepts about success and failure have been turned upside down. The resurrection leads us to reality from the side of God, and, from that side, the cross is not ultimately a failure. So the resurrection calls into question all histories of success and of failure. As historical beings we only experience in fragmented ways; yet because of the resurrection our history "stands open towards eschatological consummation: 'In hope we are redeemed.' "[57] While the positive experience of meaningfulness always takes in unredeemed conditions, there is always present to us the eschatological fact of Christ's resurrection.

For Schillebeeckx, God remains incomprehensibly positive; God never wills the negative aspects of our history. The negativity of suffering and death play an indirect role in God's providence, what is directly willed is the overcoming of all negativity. The resurrection is a manifestation of such a will, an eschatological one at that.

Suffering and the Task of Theology

According to Schillebeeckx, the fundamental question confronting our technological and secularized society is one that haunted previous generations and that the prophets posed: "Where is your God?" The question is being asked in a situation marked by intense and universal suffering which defies rational explanations. So Schillebeeckx's theology begins with a question, not an answer, nor a theory. Theology's task then is to try "to discover the human face of God and starting from there, to revive hope in a society, a humanity with a more human face...."[58] Theology will then emphasize christology and soteriology. Jesus is the parable of God's compassionate love and concern for human wholeness. He is also in his life and message a paradigm for humanity, for he provides us with the basic way to wholeness. Because Schillebeeckx begins with a question about God and our situation of suffering, his emphasis on christology has a definitive soteriological dimension. His concern is the establishment of soteriology for our own cultural situation. For Schillebeeckx God's salvific presence in Jesus Christ needs to be made manifest today as it was in the death and resurrection of Jesus. The experience of salvation is just as essential today as it was in the beginning of Christianity.

The example of Jesus who went about doing good shows that faith in the loving God demands a resistance to all suffering caused by oppression. "Apart from the church's solidarity with the sufferer, whoever or whatever that may be, their Gospel becomes impossible to believe and understand."[59] The challenge of the gospels is to authentic discipleship in every generation and in every culture. God is salvifically present in our attempts at eliminating suffering. The proclamation of salvation in a world where salvation seems to be absent requires a living remembrance of the suffering Jesus. The remembrance of the disciples (anamnesis) demands praxis.

The kind of experience that is disclosive of God is not simply one characterized as illuminating but basically one of doing: the response to the gospel must be one of praxis. Yet Christian praxis which is ordained to the future encounters everywhere the forces of evil often expressed in suffering and ultimately in death. The breakdown of praxis as it encounters evil unavoidably calls into question the disclosive presence of God in human mediation or at least of a compassionate God. In other words the limits of praxis lead to the theodicy question. The theodicy question must be grasped from the underside, i.e., from the side of those who suffer. The history of "barbarous excess" of human suffering, especially of the suffering of the innocent, cries out against too easy a justification of God. There can be no facile philosophical or theological answer.

Within the context of a radicalization of the theodicy question, the theologian's task must be characterized differently than in the past. "But whatever one thinks of contemporary theologians, one thing should be granted them: by means of a historical praxis of commitment to mysticism and politics they are trying to discover the human face of God, starting from there in order to revive hope in a society, a humanity with a more humane face."[60] The human face has already been revealed in the person of Jesus. In the person of Jesus "the divine reality proves itself to be a reality, as the one who wills good and opposes evil, the liberator from alienation."[61] In Christ salvation is neither identified nor separated from human liberation. As mediation of God's salvific immediacy, salvation has mystical and political aspects. Yet, as Schillebeeckx points out, even after the revelation of God's face in Jesus Christ, "contemplative and liberating action themselves also stand under the finite conditions of our history of suffering...."[62] "The fact that both redemption and emancipation are found within conditions of suffering gives an inner tension to any understanding of redemption and any attempt at self-liberation."[63] Suffering as an experience of contrast is characterized by both the contemplative and the practical dimensions of knowledge. A theology that is concerned with suffering will be also characterized in the same way. The theological knowledge that emerges in the experience of contrast in suffering is contemplative in nature, but also essentially practical. As a negative experience, suffering points out the limits of the passivity of contemplation; as an overwhelming experience of the refractoriness of reality, suffering leads to action toward the overcoming of suffering.

Suffering and the Human Ways of Knowing

According to Schillebeeckx: "Human suffering has a particular critical and productive epistemological force."[64] Human knowledge and knowing, while complex, has been categorized as contemplative and practical. These two dimensions of knowing are related to the various faces of nature: nature as a given to be contemplated, enjoyed ("Consider the lilies of the field") and nature to be changed and transformed ("Fill the earth and subdue it"). Yet there is an element of nature that is refractory both to contemplation and to transformation. While nature has an increasing role to play in human history, "still, there is an impassable barrier between the two; nature retains a remnant of independence and therefore also of resistance; it refuses to be incorporated entirely into the plans of our human history."[65] Nature has two faces turned simultaneously toward humanity. This twofold aspect of nature results in two possible stances: contemplating and controlling.

The epistemological value of suffering is that it is critical of and yet links these two kinds of knowledge because it has characteristics of both. Like contemplation, suffering involves being acted upon. But we do not simply "suffer" in a purely passive way; we are also impelled to struggle with it actively. And yet by nature suffering is resistant both to contemplation and to transformation. Here Schillebeeckx speaks about contrast experience. "Contrast experience . . . especially in recollection of man's/woman's actual history of accumulated suffering, has a critical cognitive value of its own, which is not reducible to a purposive technology or to the diverse forms of contemplative, aesthetic and ludic 'goal-less' knowledge."[66] Suffering's peculiar cognitive is critical of both. "It is critical vis-à-vis a purely contemplative total perception and every theoretical, unitary system because they have already accomplished universal reconciliation; but it is critical too vis-à-vis the world-manipulating knowledge of science and technology insofar as they postulate man/woman only as the controlling subject and pass over the ethical priority to which the suffering among us have a right."[67]

In its power to both criticize and bind the two forms of knowledge, contemplative and controlling knowledge, suffering is "a critical epistemological force which leads to new action, which anticipates a better future and seeks to put it into practice"[68] as an experience of contrast. The contrast experience of suffering is possible only on the basis of an implicit longing for happiness, and unjust suffering at least presupposes a vague awareness of the possible significance of human integrity. Understood in this way, action to overcome suffering is possible only through anticipation of a possible universal significance to come. "In that sense activity designed to overcome suffering is only possible by virtue of an at least implicit or confused anticipation of a possible universal meaning yet to come."[69]

Salvation and Suffering

For Schillebeeckx it is not possible to approach the basic question of salvation that lies at the core of the Christian message without attending to the experience of suffering. For, as he writes;

> "well-being" is a concept which . . . is brought to life and made intelligible only through contrasted negative experiences, conjoined with at least sporadic experiences of what "makes sense"—whence there arises in hope an anticipation of "total sense" or "hale-ness," being whole.[70]

Thus, humanity cannot know what it means to be saved without the experience of suffering and the memory of the history of all human suffering. For the desire to be saved

> presupposes an implicit craving for happiness, a craving for well-being or "making whole"; . . . a vague consciousness of what in a positive sense human integrity or wholeness should entail . . . an awareness of a positive call of and to the *humanum* . . . a positive, if so far unarticulated, feeling for value, at the same time releasing it and compelling its expression in the conscience, which begins to protest.[71]

The refractory dimension of suffering and therefore of reality frustrates every attempt by human reason to control or manipulate it. Reality resists human reason but as such, that is, in its resistance it is also revelatory since as such it "constantly directs our planning and reflection like a hidden magnet" moving us to "an ever-wider searching."[72] Thus suffering becomes the foundation of the revelation of "a transcendent power, something that comes from elsewhere."[73]

Many of the deepest insights into human nature, revelatory insights, come in moments of suffering when the reality of the present contradicts the fundamental trust undergirding one's existence. Such experience of suffering reveals the fragility of our own humanness, and our inability to bring about our own salvation. Such contrast experiences subvert any uncritical trust in the current state of things. They urge us forward to struggle for a world of greater justice. They inculcate within us a "critical negativity," a constant questioning toward everything that promised to be the fulfillment hoped for. In the overcoming of suffering our knowledge of God grows.

> What God is must emerge from our unrestrained involvement with [one another], and through building up liberating structures without which human salvation proves impossible.[74]

Such involvement remains the test of our affirmations about God:

> through and in the way in which persons live, they themselves really confirm the nature of God where (whether or not they have a religious motivation) they further good and fight evil and suffering.[75]

The experience of personal suffering and the memory of the suffering humanity and of the suffering Christ impels us toward the future in trust.

Conclusion

By starting his theology with suffering in all of its varied modes, Schillebeeckx has clearly signaled that his intention is truly ecumenical. His intention is to take seriously that all theology is fundamentally a form of inculturation: theology has to be responsible to all humanity.

To begin with suffering is to begin with a universal situation that people of good will can accept: the need of salvation. Emphasis on salvation implies praxis; praxis here will be both transformative and contemplative. In his theological method Schillebeeckx is a dialectical but not a dualistic thinker. For him there are not two spheres of immanence and transcendence any more than there are dual truths of reason and revelation. There is one reality which is more than we know.

Revelation is that specifically religious mode of experience that puts us in touch with God, with the gracious foundations of our being. Grace is always experienced as beyond our own capacities coming to us from the initiative of God and yet revealing to us our authentic self. God is revealed by revealing the human being to itself, both in its negativity and in its possibility for goodness. The Christian has a universal message for all humanity, not in the sense of disclosing something never known before, but rather in the sense of having a uniquely compelling paradigm in Jesus of that universal experience of grace: the compassion of God.

A Christian theology that begins from the perspective of suffering must focus on christology and soteriology. It will also emphasize ethics as a significant aspect of the gospel's credibility. Schillebeeckx also affirms that our knowledge of God is deepened through our ethical activity toward which recognition of our solidarity in suffering impels us. Ethical action for Schillebeeckx carries the "greatest density of revelation."

3
The Suffering of God in the Theology of Jürgen Moltmann

Introduction

Jürgen Moltmann, born in 1926 and, since 1967, professor of systematic theology at Tübingen, has become, since the publication of his *Theology of Hope* in 1964, one of the most influential of contemporary German Protestant theologians. The two basic themes of his theology—God as the power of hope, and God as the suffering one present in human suffering—can be traced to the period of 1945–1948 when he was a prisoner of war. In the midst of a desperate situation shared by millions of others, he experienced the reality of God. He himself affirms: "The 'question of God' first came to me during the fire-storm which, in July 1943, reduced my home town of Hamburg to rubble and ashes: Why have I survived this? And then with the uncovering of the German crimes at Auschwitz and Maidanel: How can one live with this?"[1]

Influential in Moltmann's understanding of theology was his sense of involvement in the suffering and guilt of the German nation. This experience led him to see theology from an ethical and political perspective. In his very influential work *The Crucified God* (1974), Moltmann brought the various elements of his experience of the reality of God and his methodological perspective together. In this book God is perceived as one involved in the suffering and despair of the world. It is here that the author points to the trinitarian nature of the cross and the redeeming power of the self-sacrificial love of the triune God. In his latest work in christology, *The Way of Jesus Christ,* Moltmann sees an emphasis on the suffering of Jesus as necessary "In order to develop a christology which is relevant in the suffering of our own time."[2]

Theology and Theodicy

While Jürgen Moltmann's theological journey has taken different turns, the central focus has remained the same. For Moltmann the goal of theology is to bring about a messianic dogmatics around the two basic doctrines of the Trinity and that of the kingdom of God.[3] Now the fundamental context of such an approach is the suffering of the world in need of liberation. Christian faith is grounded in promises of ultimate liberation from suffering. Again here the predominant question is that of theodicy. The question about God arises most profoundly from the pain of injustice in the world and from abandonment in suffering.[4]

> Man and the world are mediated today in the realm of history, and that means in social, political and technological history. Without humanization of the world, man will not find his inner identity, and without a solution to the identity crisis of modern man there is no imaginable solution to the social and political crises of the world. The theodicy question and the identity question are two sides of the same coin.[5]

For Moltmann, then, any authentic theology today must come to terms with the theodicy question, and there is no doubt that his theology represents an impressive response to the God-question as it is raised in the face of suffering. For Moltmann, the problem of suffering is not a theoretical issue for armchair theology, but one that directly concerns Christian praxis in solidarity with those who suffer.

> Sharing in the suffering of this time, Christian theology is truly contemporary theology. Whether or not it can be so depends less upon the openness of theologians and their

theories of the world and more upon whether they have
honestly and without reserve come to terms with the death
cry of Jesus for God.[6]

The theodicy question is built into the very nature of suffering. For,
"Anyone who suffers without cause first thinks that he has been forsaken by God. God seems to him to be the mysterious, incomprehensible God who destroys the good fortune that he gave."[7]

Love and the Power of Suffering

The power of suffering lies not simply in protest but because the
fundamental reason why one suffers is the fact that one loves: "The
person who can no longer love, even himself, no longer suffers, for he
is without grief, without feeling and indifferent."[8] The reality of suffering is directly connected to our ability to love and therefore to our vulnerability for "we suffer and die because and insofar as we love."[9]
Suffering can be understood in different ways: there is a suffering that
can be eliminated and another kind that cannot. For Moltmann there is
also another kind of suffering: the suffering we place on others. It is a
suffering we overcome by transferring it to others.

Yet essential to Moltmann's understanding of suffering is the
intrinsic connection between suffering and love. Within this perspective the fundamental obstacle to any understanding of suffering is that
of apathy. Apathy is understood as the spiritual sickness of contemporary society.

Life becomes inhuman; it becomes superficial. Work and
consumption have the effect of repressing suffering, one's
own as well as the other's. And when suffering is
repressed, so is love. Finally, with the loss of love, comes
the demise of interest in life. One walks over dead bodies
and one becomes a living corpse.[10]

The possibility of suffering is an essential element of the will to
live. So according to Moltmann, "The ideal of Western progress—to
lead a life free from pain or suffering—is intolerable because it inflicts
suffering and pain on others."[11] The ideal of a life without suffering
leads to the oppression of others.[12]

It is within the context of apathy that Christianity must proclaim its message. It must do so in two different ways. First, by emphasizing that helplessness can be overcome. "There will be no survival for mankind without the rebirth of the power of hope, which in the face of the possibility of the world's death wills to live and prepares to live." And, second, by accepting that suffering is part of human existence. For the attempt to eliminate all suffering usually is "at the cost of increased suffering for other people."

> The ideal of a life without suffering makes one group of people apathetic and brutal towards other groups, which are supposed to pay the price. The shifting of the cost on to other people is intolerable for both.[13]

But the suffering of the innocent can never be justified. No theodicy can do justice to that type of suffering. Only a hope in a future salvation can be offered; no theoretical explanation will do. The suffering of the innocent challenges any claims to God's righteousness in the world; such a claim must remain an open question to be answered in the future. In the present, such suffering must be responded to by protest and not by resignation. An answer to suffering must issue in liberating praxis.

Suffering and the Theology of the Cross

From the very beginning Moltmann's theology has given prominence to the question of God's righteousness in the face of suffering such as that of Auschwitz. One could say that the first phase of his theodicy could be characterized as an eschatological one that emphasizes the resurrection but gives no explanation of suffering, but yet provides some form of hope in God's ultimate victory. In a second phase, one emphasizing the cross, there is the additional theme of God's loving solidarity with the suffering world. There is here a movement from the resurrection as the event of God's promise, to the cross as the event of God's love. The basic idea of the second phase is that of a compassionate love, a love which suffers in solidarity with those who suffer. The cross does not solve the problem of suffering but meets it with voluntary solidarity which does not abolish suffering but overcomes what Moltmann calls the "suffering in suffering": the lack of love, the abandonment in suffering. The basic questions a theologian must face are the following: What gives hope in God's promised kingdom in face of innocent suffering? How is it possible to continue to love and hope in the midst of repeated disappointments, suffering, and death?

With suffering as the point of departure for his theology, Moltmann develops his own understanding of what theology should be. Two basic questions govern Moltmann's understanding of the nature of theology: What makes any theology be a Christian theology, and how and in what ways can a Christian theology become a critical theology? For Moltmann, Christian theology is a theology of the cross, and because it is a theology of the cross, it is critical theology.

In the first part of this answer, Moltmann is directly dependent on Luther. Following Luther, Moltmann affirms that "the Cross is the criterion of all things."[14] Luther had contrasted his theology of the cross (*theologia crucis*) with the prevalent theology: the theology of glory (*theologia gloriae*). These two theologies represent two different ways of knowing God: the theology of glory knows God through his power as that is manifested in creation; the other knows God as hidden in the suffering and humiliation of the cross. Such a knowledge of God can never be misused. All human expectation about God and God's attributes are shattered on the cross, for on the cross God is not revealed in power but in its opposite—in powerlessness.

> To know God in the cross of Christ is a crucifying form of knowledge, because it shatters everything to which a man can hold and on which he can build, both his works and his knowledge of reality, and precisely in so doing sets us free.[15]

Following Luther, the cross is the decisive epistemological criterion for our knowledge of God; the cross is the end of the kind of theology that has been prevalent up to now and the beginning of a specifically Christian theology.

> Either Jesus who was abandoned by God is the end of all theology or he is the beginning of a specifically Christian and therefore critical and liberating, theology and life.[16]

We must then say about our knowledge of God:

> So God is not known through his works in reality, but through his suffering in the passiveness of faith, which allows God to work on it; killing in order to make alive, judging in order to set free. So his knowledge is achieved not by the guiding thread of analogies from earth to heaven, but on the contrary, through contradiction, sorrow and suffering.[17]

The Christian understanding of God has its roots in an historical event: the cross. The way of history is the way of the cross, and the cross is the way into the trinitarian God. It is not creation that leads us to God, but the cross.

So God is known in and through history; God's attributes are historically revealed and cannot simply be deduced from nature, so that it is impossible to think of God apart from history. For Moltmann, the cross of Christ represents the overthrow of political-religious forms claiming power, meaning, and value in our lives and in our world. In his cross Jesus was identified with the present reality of the world in all its negativity: its subjection to sin, suffering, and death. The resurrection constitutes God's opposition to this situation, and since both occurred in the same person of Jesus Christ, the paschal mystery represents a dialectical understanding of God's presence/love in our world. The dialectic of cross and resurrection gives Moltmann's theology a strongly christological center in the particular history of Jesus.

The Cross and Political Theology

A Christian theology centered on the cross involves a transition from pure theory to critical theory. In this transition, Moltmann is borrowing from the critical theory of the Frankfurt school. This school's emphasis on negative dialectics fits well Moltmann's concern with the iconoclastic role of the cross. The cross unmasks all idols and ideologies.

> Because of its subject, the theology of the cross, right
> down to its method and practice, can only be polemical,
> dialectical, antithetical and critical theory.[18]

As a critical theory of God, the cross tells us of the character of God's presence in the cross of Jesus and refuses to accept the traditional theistic idea of an apathetic God. The affirmation of the pathos of God leads to a theory of God that refutes the idols of security and the status quo.[19] And an apathetic God leads to an apathetic anthropology.

As a critical theory, the theology of the cross leads to a praxis approach to faith. Moltmann has expressed his adherence to the program of political theology which he prefers to call a "political theology of hope." Political theology, according to Moltmann, "designates the field, the milieu, the environment, and the medium in which Christian theology shall be articulated today."[20] Human destiny has become increasingly linked with politics, and this is the sphere in which the question of God's promise and human liberation must be raised. The field of politics extends to basically all the constructive and destructive possibilities of human existence.[21] Political theology in its hermeneutical function moves beyond pure understanding of biblical texts to the transformation of the world of suffering.[22]

As previously stated, the cross of Christ is the source and the criterion for a political theology.[23] So a theology of the cross does not lead simply to negation but involves also transformation. Negativity cannot characterize Christianity's relation to the world.[24] While the cross is still with us and the kingdom of God is still expected, the Christian stance cannot be one of passive waiting. "Though this world is not yet the Kingdom of God itself, it is the battleground and the construction site for the Kingdom which came in earlier from God himself."[25] So a political theology "wants to bring the Christians, *as Christians*, that is, as *liberators,* to the place where they are being waited upon by the crucified one. In the suffering and condemned ones of this earth Christ is waiting upon his own and their presence."[26]

Suffering and Liberation

Moltmann's position relative to God's suffering on the cross is concerned with the question of power, the power of God's suffering love to overcome suffering. The implication of Moltmann's position is that the suffering of love has the power to liberate from suffering. "This means that through his suffering he liberates those who are suffering: through his weakness he gains peace in the world; through his God-forsakenness he brings God to the forsaken; through his death he creates salvation for those condemned to death."[27] God's power, according to Moltmann, does not lie in his suppression of suffering, but in his embracing suffering out of love. God's solidarity with those who suffer does not abolish suffering: it eliminates the suffering in suffering.

> For the suffering in suffering is the lack of love, and the wounds in wounds are the abandonment, and the powerlessness in pain is unbelief. And therefore the suffering of abandonment is overcome by the suffering of love, which is not afraid of what is sick and ugly, but accepts it and takes it to itself in order to heal it.[28]

The divine overcoming of suffering can be participated in through discipleship and the following of the crucified Christ. There is present here a certain mysticism of suffering: suffering is overcome by suffering and wounds are healed by wounds. The tragedy of suffering is met with the suffering of love.

The Suffering of God

Moltmann combines the theology of the cross derived from Luther's with a critical theory borrowed from the Frankfurt school to arrive at a dialectic on the cross—God is revealed in God's opposite, the cross. God is perceived in paradox; through dialectics and not analogy. For Moltmann, God is revealed in the God-forsakenness experience by the one who had experience—God as "Abba." Absence is affirmed as presence.

The bottom line for Moltmann is that contemporary Christian theology must be able to formulate its doctrine of God in such a way that it takes account of the suffering of the world. Now a revolution in the concept of God must lead ultimately to a God who participates in the suffering of creation. In the mystery of the cross God is not simply to be set over against suffering; the cross reveals that suffering is in God. Moltmann understands the cross as a divine event, "as an event between Jesus and his God and Father."[29] When understood in such a way, "the form of the crucified Christ is the Trinity."[30] In his work on christology, Moltmann sums up his theology of the cross in the following way:

> The Father suffers the death of the Son. He suffers it in the infinite pain of his love for the Son. The death of the Son therefore corresponds to the pain of the Father. And when in this descent into hell the Son loses sight of the Father, then in this judgment the Father also loses sight of the Son. Here what is at stake is the divine consistency, the inner life of the Trinity. Here the self-communicating love of the Father becomes infinite pain over the death of the Son. Here the responding love of the Son turns into infinite suffering over his forsakenness by the Father. What happens on Golgotha reaches into the very depths of the Godhead and therefore puts its impress on the trinitarian life of God in eternity. In Christian faith the cross is always at the centre of the Trinity, for the cross reveals the heart of the triune God, which beats for his whole creation.[31]

The emphasis is on the forsakenness of Jesus by God, yet the Father forsakes the Son for us in order to become the God and Father of the forsaken. At the same time, "the son is surrendered to this death in order to become the brother and Saviour of all the men and women who are condemned and accursed."[32]

But the Son is not simply surrendered by the Father: the Son, according to Philippians 2, deliberately chose the way of suffering. According to Moltmann, the sufferings of Christ "are part of the history of suffering endured by Israel and God's prophets."[33] Jesus' sufferings "are open for fellowship," a fellowship experienced by untold generations. What is paradoxical about Jesus' suffering is that he suffered most intensely from the forsakenness by the Father. And yet on the cross there is truly a community of wills: the kenosis of the Father and of the Son: "The surrender of the Father and the Son is made through 'the Spirit.' "[34] For Moltmann, the Spirit also suffers in the suffering of Christ, for there is also a kenosis of the Spirit.

The fundamental answer given to those who suffer is that God also suffers. For Jesus' weakness and death are also the weakness and death of God. The human suffering of Jesus is the divine suffering of God.[35]

The Theology of the Pain of God

So a theology of the cross must be understood as a "theology of the pain of God, which means the theology of the divine co-suffering or compassion."[36] God is not the cause of Christ's suffering and Christ is not simply a victim. Kenosis as surrender of self is always characterized by freedom. Moltmann sums up his understanding of the suffering God in the following way:

> "The sufferings of Christ" are God's sufferings because through them God shows his solidarity with human beings and his whole creation everywhere: *God is with us.*
>
> "The sufferings of Christ" are God's sufferings because through them God intervenes vicariously on our behalf, saving us at the point where we are unable to stand but are forced to sink into nothingness: *God is for us.*
>
> "The sufferings of Christ" are God's sufferings, finally, because out of them the new creation of all things is born: *we come from God.*[37]

So there is a divine dimension to Christ's suffering and it expresses itself as a power of solidarity and leads to a new creation. In Christ, God experiences history, vulnerability, and even death "in order to heal, to liberate and to confer new life."[38] It is specific to Christianity's understanding of God that God is one who suffers. For "a God who cannot suffer is poorer than any man . . . a God who is incapable of suffering is a being who cannot be involved."[39] So it must be the loving nature of God that must be emphasized and not God's omnipotence.

Political theology as critical theology must find its roots in a deeper theological treatment of the problem of suffering. There can be no deeper theological understanding of suffering than positing suffering in God, and God in suffering, and expressing this position through the symbol of the Trinity. The Trinity includes all human and divine suffering into one symbol.[40] Because the inner life of God embraces suffering, Moltmann speaks of suffering as having an aspect of eternity to it. "With the surrender of the Son to death on the cross, the endless suffering of God begins."[41]

God's Suffering and Human Suffering

What can a theology of the cross mean for those who suffer? As Moltmann often affirms, "anyone who suffers without cause first thinks that he has been forsaken by God."[42] For a theology of the cross, God and suffering do not stand in contradiction of one another. Since God is love, the loving God who can suffer and does is also the basic source of any meaning suffering may have. For as Moltmann writes, "The believer really participates in the suffering of God in the world, because he partakes in the suffering of the love of God."[43] It is because it is God's nature to be compassionate that we can participate in God's suffering and therefore in the suffering of the world.[44] God is revealed to us in the suffering of the cross; but it is also because we suffer that God's self is revealed to us. It is because of this that the cross is a scandal; it is a scandal of a God who is compassionate to the extremes. God's compassion revealed in the cross is emancipative. "The free acceptance of suffering in behalf of others is the transfiguration of suffering. 'I' is no longer destructive; rather 'I' unites. It does not isolate anymore. It binds together."[45]

While Jesus' suffering in solidarity with us has brought about reconciliation, "each of us has waiting for us in our lives a measure of suffering which we are called upon to assume in solidarity with all who suffer."[46] Solidarity in suffering is for the purpose of liberation. "God's pain in the world is the way to God's happiness with the world."[47] Fellowship in the joy won through God's liberating suffering leads into suffering for the liberation of others.[48]

Eschatology and Suffering

Since this liberation is still in process and is not fully realized, the theodicy question is still an open-ended one. Christ is still suffering in those who suffer. Moltmann writes about the apocalyptic suffering of Christ: "The apocalyptic Christ suffers in the victims of sin and violence. The apocalyptic Christ suffers and sighs too in the tormented creation sighing under the violent acts of our modern human civilization." Jesus did not simply suffer for himself; he suffered for the world. "In 'the sufferings of Christ' the end-time sufferings of the whole world are anticipated and vicariously experienced." However the "sufferings of Christ" are not simply Christ's own personal suffering, but include the sufferings of those who have suffered, and now suffer, for Christ's sake.

> Understood apocalyptically, the kingdom of God brings the end of this world-time and the beginning of the new creation. That is to say, its coming brings the tribulations and assailments of the end-time. For "this world," they mean the catastrophic end. But in fact they are the birth pangs of the new world. These "worlds" are "world era," aeons, not heaven and earth themselves. Liberation from "the godless ties of this world" frees people for "grateful service" on behalf of "all those whom God has created."[49]

Moltmann's approach to suffering is clearly marked by his understanding of eschatology. By his focusing on the biblical promises of a new creation, Moltmann developed eschatology "as the doctrine of hope that is founded on Christ, that embraces temporal life and the cosmos and that is oriented toward the future of the kingdom of God." Moltmann characterizes his basic theological position as "eschatological christology." The suffering of this world and the meaning that can be given to it are affected by Moltmann's eschatological perspective.

Conclusion

Moltmann's theology is oriented both to praxis and doxology—i.e. theology is not only interested in transformation but also in contemplation and celebration. Praxis itself is distorted into activism unless there is also enjoyment of being and praise of God, not only for what he has done, but also for what he is. Theological knowing can never imitate technological knowing in its dominating drive.

Moltmann's theology is characterized by its openness to dialogue. Such an openness is inherent to the very structure of his theology which is characterized by an eschatological perspective. Moltmann's most important contribution has been his ability to accept with utmost seriousness suffering in all of its forms. His radical interpretations of the paschal mystery and the trinitarian mystery have had important implications for contemporary theology. His recovery of the fullness of biblical eschatology has led him to what he has coined a "christology in the eschatological history of God."[50] Eschatological history is "history under the promise of life." Moltmann's answer to the problem of suffering is "christology on the road" which is also "a christology beneath the cross."[51] Yet such a "christology" is not without some problems.

Moltmann's theology of suffering has been criticized from two perspectives: the eschatological and the trinitarian. These two aspects cannot be fully separated since if suffering is taken up by God, such suffering should ultimately be eliminated. The most controversial point in Moltmann's position is his affirmation that the suffering God in some way causes the suffering of his Son. Schillebeeckx, who maintains God's absolute support for Jesus in life and death, criticizes Moltmann's position as one that eternalizes suffering in God and therefore leads to a false soteriology.[52] Moltmann is accused of providing a solution to the theodicy problem that involves a transcendent ontologization of suffering and evil. Dorothy Soelle has also protested against Moltmann's perception of God as causing suffering directly, especially the suffering of the Son. According to Dorothy Soelle, "Moltmann attempts to develop a 'theology of the cross' from the perspective of the one who originates and causes suffering."[53] A broader criticism has been directed to all "suffering God" theologies. They are accused of continuing in new forms the traditional piety that sanctions suffering as imitation of the Holy One. Because God suffers and God is good, we are also good if we suffer.

There are resources in Moltmann's theology for meeting these objections. For Moltmann, all language of "forsakenness" relative to

God's relationship to Jesus on the cross is misunderstood unless it is grasped as being *"the theology of the pain of God,* which means the theology of *the divine co-suffering or compassion."*[54] The whole thrust of Moltmann's position is his understanding of love. "God is love; that means God is self-giving. It means God exists for us: on the cross."[55] Suffering for Moltmann does not denote a deficiency in God, but the empathy of love. God knows the suffering of passionate love. For Moltmann, Jesus and the Father can never be separated, one being the object and the other the subject: both are object and subject. They are never opposed or divided, so that the kenosis of the Son must always be the kenosis of the Father. For Moltmann there can be no question of perceiving the Father permitting, wishing Jesus' death as an appeasing sacrifice, nor of being absent on the cross. God, for Moltmann, is a suffering God. Again, according to Moltmann, Jesus "was betrayed, condemned and murdered by human beings and *God protests* against Jesus' death by raising him from the dead. Through the resurrection, God confutes Jesus' betrayers, judges and executioners."[56]

Yet Moltmann's theology of the cross and therefore of suffering cannot fully escape the accusation of being at times somewhat mystifying and open to misunderstanding. Moltmann's language about "God against God," of the infinite gulf existing between Jesus and the Father, can be misunderstood. This is especially true of Jesus' experience of abandonment on the part of the Father. The tension involved in Moltmann's position is made clearer when those who suffer without cause also experience the abandonment of God and that that experience, according to Moltmann, corresponds to the reality, since God allows evil to take its course and does not intervene to prevent suffering. So the creator responsible ultimately for the kind of world we live in; and who therefore must somehow bear responsibility for the suffering of this world, shares in the suffering of this world. Yet it is difficult to grasp how such a God can be the ground for hope for the cessation of suffering.

So it would seem that, for Moltmann, the theodicy question remains an open question until the eschaton. Emphasis on the eschatological, on the basic hope that, notwithstanding the immensity of the world's suffering, God will ultimately triumph, can easily trivialize human effort in the suppression of the causes of suffering. Part of Moltmann's response consists in the rejection of an either/or approach:

neither God alone nor man/woman alone. Yet too much emphasis on eschatology tends to a discontinuity between the past and the future. If man's/woman's actions truly count for the good or for the bad, then even God cannot overcome the past. God, for Moltmann, is such that he can even re-create the past.

This eschatological bent also influences his understanding of political theology. In light of his concept of God's future, Moltmann seems to think that politics, since it is always conflicting, is ultimate.

> Someday there will really come, out of the written word of
> the promise, the new reality. One day we shall no longer
> encounter trial and contradiction in nature, history and
> political life, but shall arrive at harmony with them.[57]

In a sense politics still abide because the kingdom of God has not yet been realized. For Moltmann political power is always ultimately one that alienates, and therefore somehow negative. So in a sense, for Moltmann, political power seems to be opposed to the kingdom of God; it is another form of negativity that is in need of being overcome. So in a political theology that is truly related to the question of suffering, human suffering should not be connected with political power but with specific oppressive forms of political power. With his understanding of political power, it is not surprising that Moltmann is not favorable to the church's involvement with politics. There is a sense here that the church is too much of the kingdom of God to be involved in the political arena.

> The church therefore must not regard itself just as a means
> to an end, but it must demonstrate already in its present
> existence that free and redeemed being with others which it
> seeks to serve. In this sense—and only in this sense—the
> church is already an end in itself . . . a congregation of the
> liberated. In that sense the church's function reaches
> beyond rendering assistance to the troubled world; it
> already possesses its own demonstrative value of being.[58]

It is then understandable that for Moltmann precision in the concepts and goals of political theology is needed. Explicit and appropriate analysis of political, social and psychological structures is necessary if a political theology is to address the question of suffering in the world. Too much focusing on the future can lead to the neglect of the present. Yet in Moltmann's latest work, there is a sense of a more realistic understanding of the church's role in the liberation of man and woman. There is much of value in Moltmann's political theology, for it does provide a vision of the future. Yet it does seem that evil and the suffering of the innocent are more radical than Moltmann perceives them. Ultimately only those who perceive the situation as it actually is can help.

4
Theology and Suffering After the End of Idealism: Johannes B. Metz

Introduction

Johannes B. Metz, professor of fundamental theology at the Westfaelische Wilhems-Universitaet, Münster, West Germany, has developed a theology within a cultural context marked by a radical individualism and in the aftermath of Auschwitz. Metz's emphasis on the negative elements of our actual situation, especially the overwhelming presence of suffering brought by human freedom gone amiss, has its roots in personal experience. Traumatic experiences as a young soldier during World War II and the silence of the German people relative to the holocaust raised for him the formal theodicy question about the suffering of the innocent. These events forced him to wrestle with fundamental questions about a Christianity and about the nature and value of a culture that could allow such atrocities and remain silent. For Metz all contemporary theology must face the "Auschwitz challenge," for Auschwitz, in its paradigmatic character, stands for the end of the modern era. As Metz writes:

> There is no meaning which one could salvage by turning one's back on Auschwitz, and no truth which one could thereby defend. Theology therefore has to make an about-

turn, a turn which will bring us face-to-face with the suffering and the victims.[1]

Auschwitz is paradigmatic of the evil that is still deeply embedded in our society, and an ongoing challenge to any attempt at explaining away suffering. There is an ongoing tendency on our part to filter out the importance of suffering in history. As Metz writes:

> We tend, consciously or unconsciously, to define history as the history of what has prevailed, as the history of the successful and the established: in historical studies, too, a kind of Darwinism in the sense of the principle of selection (*"Vae victis!"*) tends to prevail. Again it is of decisive importance that a kind of *anti-history* should develop out of the memory of suffering—an understanding of history in which the vanquished and destroyed alternatives would also be taken into account: an understanding of history *ex memoria passionis* as a history of the vanquished.[2]

At the same time and because of our cultural biases, there is a constant unwillingness on our part to grasp the cognitive and practical function of suffering. Our culture is dominated by the cult of scientific knowledge which perceives itself as a dominative form of knowledge. Yet in the context of Auschwitz dominative knowledge leads to domination, and so what is needed is a challenge to scientific knowledge. "Hence it is significant that there should be a kind of *anti-history ex memoria passionis* forming in our society, in which the existing identification of 'praxis' with 'domination of nature' is banished."[3] Not only is suffering a challenge to scientific knowledge, but it also challenges teleology and ontology. "It also seems to me important to stress the *anti-teleological* and *anti-ontological* character of suffering—not least of all as against certain tendencies within theology itself."[4] Suffering resists a too facile reconciliation of human reality and nature. In fact, "suffering" emphasizes the contrast between nature and history, between teleology and eschatology. There is no "objective" reconciliation between them, no obvious, manageable unity.[5] Influenced by the thought of Theodor Adorno, Metz affirms:

> The least trace of meaningless suffering in the world we
> experience cancels all affirmative ontology and all teleolo-
> gy as untrue, and exposes them as a mythology of modern
> times.[6]

Emphasis on the cognitive and practical function of suffering will
affect the nature of theology. Theology will by necessity be political.
Metz goes on to describe such a theology.[7]

> This political theology after Auschwitz is not a theology in
> terms of a system. It is theology in terms of human sub-
> jects, with a practical foundation. It continually introduces
> into public awareness "the struggle for recollection," for
> the recollecting knowledge which is related to the human
> subjects concerned.[8]

Such a theology will focus on the theodicy question, not in an individualistic way, but in a political form.[9]

Political theology originates as a critique of contemporary individualism, and of the conformity of the bourgeoisie. The primary purpose of a political theology is to be critical and transformative as a
reflection and critique of the socio-political constitution of human life
and the Christian tradition. Here the whole reality of suffering "interrupts" all of our theological construing and theorizing and necessitates
action. Here history is revealed not primarily as the history of success
but as a history of suffering, of failure. Here Christ is identified with
the history of suffering.

Suffering, according to political theology, relocates theology on
the side of solidarity and praxis, and emphasizes that faith means primarily the struggle for transformation over and above that of personal
decision. It must address the overwhelming problem of massive public
suffering that makes pure theoretical understanding impossible and,
ultimately, anti-human. Since suffering is very concrete, very much
there, it forces all theological, historical, and social categories to be
concrete.

By emphasizing suffering as the interpretative framework for
any contemporary anthropology, political theology intends to criticize
and transform the *epistemic* and *genetic* nature of modern conscious-

ness, which is perceived as fundamentally disturbed. The basic consciousness of modernity is the consciousness of the bourgeois. Political theology wants to emphasize that such a consciousness can be criticized only if the consciousness that has primacy is that of the one who suffers. What is feared in our contemporary culture is, according to Metz,

> the silent disappearance of the subject and the death of the individual in the anonymous compulsions and structures of a world that is constructed of unfeeling rationality and consequently allows identity, memory and consciousness of the human soul to become "extinct."[10]

Suffering and Technological Mentality

The dominative nature of knowing brought about by the turn to technology has brought about a distortion of historical consciousness where timelessness becomes the only category so that neither past nor future has any importance. "The modern world, with its technical civilization, is not simply a rational universe. Its myth is evolution. The silent interest of its rationality is the fiction of time as empty infinity, which is free of surprises and within which everyone and everything is enclosed without grace."[11] The loss of memory as a faculty for the past is conducive to the inability on the part of individuals to grieve or to feel guilty.

What J.B. Metz criticizes about culture, he also criticizes about Christianity. Only a radical conversion and radical therapy can save Christianity from detrimental forgetfulness. According to Metz, the real purpose of a converted Christianity is to take the side of the sufferer and to do this by retrieving the dangerous memory of Jesus Christ.[12] According to Metz:

> The substratum of history, then, is not nature as evolution or a process without reference to the subject. The natural history of man is to some extent the history of his suffering ... The essential dynamics of history consist of the memory of suffering as a negative consciousness of future free-

dom and as a stimulus to overcome suffering within the framework of that freedom. The history of freedom is therefore—subject to the assumed alienation of man and nature—only possible as a history of suffering.[13]

The sufferer, the failed human existence, forgotten, erupts and interrupts the forgetfulness of our contemporary culture and religion. In the experience of suffering lies the yearning for a different world, the seeds of hope and a concern for the future.

Suffering and Political Theology

In response to the cultural and ecclesial situations, J.B. Metz has developed and advocated a political theology.

Political theology seeks to make contemporary theologians aware that a trial is pending between the eschatological message of Jesus and the socio-political reality. It insists on the permanent relation to the world inherent in the salvation merited by Jesus, a relation not to be understood in a natural-cosmological but in a socio-political sense; that is, as a critical, liberating force in regard to the social world and its historical process.[14]

Christian theology is necessarily political since its object is the God of salvation revealed and made manifest in the person of Jesus Christ. The salvation proclaimed by Jesus concerns not only the spiritual existence of individuals but also the social and historical dimensions of the world. In fact, salvation is mediated through history, and salvific grace is fundamentally a social reality, so that world history is not separate from salvation history. Christianity must be political to avoid the danger of individualism and privatization. A history without salvation or a salvation outside of history leads to a false dualism or to gnosticism. To think in terms of two histories, one natural and one supernatural, undermines the value of human existence. A world history that is not salvation history is simply a transition without value, especially when such a history is marked by suffering and death.

The presupposition of Metz's theology is that the world is to be understood historically as the consequence and product of human activity. The world is not "nature"; nature is simply that which affords the raw matter for human history. So great is the distance from nature to history that Metz can say concerning the world as nature that a "cosmological atheism" is justified.

For Metz any reconciliation between nature and man/woman is ultimately utopian and bound to fail. The existence of suffering opposes such a reconciliation. "Suffering brings out the contrast between nature and history, between teleology and eschatology."[15] In fact, for Metz, "The smallest trace of meaningless suffering in the world we experience gives the lie to this whole affirmative ontology and all our teleology and unmasks them as modern mythology."[16]

Political Theology and Salvation

J.B. Metz perceives his political theology as a corrective to previous theologies and as a way to give reason for his faith in the salvific value of the Christian reality. Many soteriologies that do take suffering seriously are criticized by Metz as inadequate. He criticizes Karl Rahner's transcendental approach because it is not historically concrete enough and therefore does not value enough the history of suffering. Metz also resists J. Moltmann's understanding of suffering as an intra-trinitarian event. The history of suffering must be accepted in all of its concreteness and cannot be covered up.

So the actual task of political theology is to criticize existing ideologies, secular or religious, by emphasizing the cognitive and practical function of theology. Its goal is to be an aid to the church in becoming a critic of society by developing a critical corrective to utopianism. Theology simply cannot exist in an abstract context. Theology must focus critical attention upon concrete subjects and the global, historical processes which have formed them. Theology in its most fundamental dimension must be a political theology of the subject and must acknowledge the primacy of praxis.[17] The hermeneutical process must pay attention to the ethical and social implications of the major religious symbols in Christianity. It must be wary of too facile a translation of salvation as emancipation, for emancipation must be tested in the concreteness of history and society. Only those understandings of redemption as emancipation can be considered true which do not dissolve or dismiss the real history of suffering.

The emphasis on suffering reveals that the authentic human subject is one with a past and a future, and that authentic human freedom is connected to suffering. In fact, human identity is caught up with the possibility to remember the past, and in a special way the past history of suffering. Human historical identity is intimately related to "the freedom to suffer the suffering of others and to respect the prophecy of others' suffering, even though the negative aspect of suffering seems to be forbidden."[18]

Human freedom that eliminates suffering from its scope is on its way to totalitarianism. In the freedom to suffer emerges also the freedom to hope and "any society that ignores or thrusts into the background these aspects of the history of freedom must pay for this neglect by gradually losing its own visible freedom."[19]

Memory and Suffering

Within the dialectics of freedom in suffering and hope, Metz considers the essential structures of historical consciousness: memory, narrative, and solidarity. These three structures are inter-connected. "Memory and narrative only have a practical character when they are considered together with solidarity, and solidarity has no specifically cognitive status without memory and narrative."[20] Memory is a constitutive element of human identity. Memory here cannot be identified simply with nostalgia for a utopian past from which all negative elements have been removed. Established institutions seem constantly to eradicate memories of suffering; they fear the subversive content of such memories. For Metz, memories provide men and women with a challenge not simply to dwell in the past, but to look to the future in hope. So the future is not radical or absolute; it is always qualified by the past. For Christianity, this past is the memory of Jesus Christ. Following such authors as Adorno and Habermas, Metz stresses the important role of memory in the process of knowing. In fact no actual question can be asked where the memory of the past does not obtrude. For Metz, "memory is the medium by which reason becomes practical as freedom."[21]

The Dangerous Memory of the Passion

What is most important in Metz's thought is his understanding of the role of what he calls "dangerous memory" and within the Christian tradition the memory of the crucified Lord, the *memoria passionis*. Memory itself can be co-opted to serve false ideologies, but there are

> dangerous memories, memories which make demands on us. There are memories in which earlier experiences break through to the centre-point of our lives and reveal new and dangerous insights for the present. They illuminate for a few moments and with a harsh steady light the questionable nature of things we have apparently come to terms with and show up the banality of our supposed "realism." They break through the canon of all that is taken as self-evident, and unmask as deception the certainty of those "whose hour is always there" (Jn. 7:6). They seem to subvert our structures of plausibility. Such memories are like dangerous and incalculable visitants from the past. They are memories we have to take into account; memories, as it were, with future content.[22]

Dangerous memories have the ability to disclose important and crucial insights for the present. They point out the precariousness of those realities we have come to accept as never-ending.

Dangerous memories serve to constitute the subject as subject; they are directed against all one-dimensional institutions and totalitarian structures, and are opposed by totalitarian structures.

> The enslavement of men begins when their memories of the past are taken away. All forms of colonization are based on this principle. Every rebellion against suffering is fed by the subversive power of remembered suffering. In this sense, suffering is in no way a purely passive, inactive "virtue." It is, or can be, the source of socially emancipatory action. And in this sense the memory of accumulated suffering continues to resist the cynics of modern political power.[23]

Christianity's foundations lie in a dangerous memory: the memory of the crucified Lord. This memory provides Christianity with the will to change the present: it calls it to oppose all totalitarian forces. The *memoria Christi* is the power which keeps the Christian faith alive; it is a liberating force for the freedom of the human spirit.

Narrative and Suffering

So the basic structure of faith is remembrance: faith comes to us as the personal appropriation of the memories of a specific community located in time and space. Such memories are handed down in narratives. Narrative for Metz is another essential structure of human existence. Narratives give human existence the atemporal framework; they shape individuals and societies and constitute the essence of tradition as they bring about solidarity and communion.

Narrative becomes a fundamental mode of expression for faith, for only through narrative can history and salvation somehow come together. So Christianity is a story-telling community; the "dangerous memory" of Christ's suffering is handed down in narratives. This has important consequences for Christian theology and faith and the conceptualization of salvation.

> From the outset, Christianity as a community of redeemed in Jesus Christ is not primarily a community of interpretation and of argumentation but a community of remembrance and of narrative; a narrating remembrance of the passion, death, and resurrection of Jesus. The Logos of the cross and resurrection has an indispensable narrative structure. The communication of the experience of faith as of every original experience of something new, something never before present, does not have the form of argument but of narrative.[24]

Social change cannot simply be brought about by pure rational discourse. Stories of suffering, dangerous memories, resist purely rational arguments. Narratives make it possible for history to be read again and again and again. Narratives have certain characteristics that make it possible for them to be vehicles of change. In narrative there is a direct connection between expression and lived experience, between "word" and "act." Again another aspect of narrative is that usually marginal groups use stories as a mode of communication. These marginal groups use narratives with a "practical and socially critical effect and with a dangerous and liberating intention."[25]

While the Christian faith has a narrative structure, faith also is characterized by an argumentative and rational element. In fact, the rational element is there to protect the integrity of the narrative. Metz describes the role of rational argument—"the primary function of which is to protect the narrative memory of salvation in a scientific world, to allow it to be at stake and to prepare the way for a renewal of this narrative, without which the experience of salvation is silenced."[26] And yet since what is essential to the theological process is a history of suffering, "the category of narrative memory prevents salvation and redemption from becoming paradoxically unhistorical and does not subordinate them to the logical identity of argumentational mediation."[27]

Solidarity and Suffering

One of the basic consequences of the narrative nature of Christianity is that narrativity always issues in solidarity. Narratives demand participation: while certain languages such as dogmatic language are languages *spoken to* an audience, narrative is a language *spoken with* an audience. The audience become active subjects of the language. Narratives are constitutive of the historical and personal subject. Narratives have the capacity to bring about solidarity with others of the past and the present, especially solidarity with "the suffering other." Solidarity has been defined by Rebecca Chopp as "the timefulness of belonging to our memories and our future, the timefulness of suffering with and for others, the timefulness of freedom and intersubjectivity."[28] For Metz, the solidarity brought about by the Christian narratives "is simultaneously mystical and universal as well as political and particular."[29]

Memory, narrative, and solidarity function together and focus attention upon the interruptive power of Christian praxis."[30] The "dangerous memory" of the Crucified Christ embedded in narratives offers inspiration for a new form of solidarity with, and of responsibility

towards, those most distant from us. The history of those who have
suffered and now suffer unites all men/women like a second nature.

For Metz "solidarity is above all a category of help, support, and
togetherness, by which the subject, suffering acutely and threatened,
can be raised up."[31] Solidarity is for the purpose of the overcoming of
suffering caused by oppression and injustice. "It is in this solidarity
that memory and narrative (of salvation) acquire their specific mystical
and political praxis."[32] In fact, without solidarity neither memory nor
narrative function properly as "practical categories of theology."[33]

Solidarity and Anthropology

As suffering reveals the distortion of anthropology, so it provides
the constructive reformulation of anthropology and Christianity
through solidarity with those who suffer. Solidarity is the most fundamental category of anthropology, ontologically both in terms of the
underlying structures of being and in terms of actual sensuous being.
Solidarity implies not only that our lives are interwoven with the living
but also that we are intrinsically connected to the dead.
Intersubjectivity is the primary characteristic of individual life, and life
as a whole; there are no pure individual categories for meaning, for
freedom, or even for reason. As Gabriel Marcel wrote: "A complete
and concrete knowledge of oneself cannot be egocentric; however
paradoxical it may seem, I should prefer to say that it must be hetero-
centric. The fact is that we can understand ourselves by starting from
the other, or from others, and only by starting from them."[34]

Suffering and Communication

Language as sign has an ontological as well as a descriptive purpose. It extends our vision of reality and initiates a process of fuller
realization of self. Processes of self-understanding and self-realization
are intertwined. Self-realization can be realized even when the context
of self-understanding is obscured. The escape from meaninglessness is
achievable through the transcendence of the act of dialogue. The
importance of the dialogue is that it brings into consciousness a sense
of the actuality of suffering. Dialogue introduces additional possibilities for the determination of the deeper understanding of suffering. In

dialogue there is a reaching-out for a plenitude of meaning in suffering. The phase of dialogue cannot be skipped as if it were possible to do away immediately with the suffering. Without dialogue there can be no change; causes of suffering can be eliminated from the outside, but not suffering, since it is by essence interpersonal. In dialogue the sufferer finds solidarity, and solidarity is already a victory over suffering.

This solidarity is not simply a present reality. There is an historical dimension to it. While solidarity constitutes an ongoing community of interpretation, it is also constitutive of an historical community of interpretation which transmits present interpretation to future generations. Past sufferings are not remedies for themselves but give the ongoing community new hope in the present and for the future. Past memories are not simply recalled but they are reinterpreted, reconceived, accepted and lived within the present.

Suffering and Praxis

Solidarity, then, for Metz is a fundamental structure of human existence. Intersubjectivity and interdependence characterize the lives of men and women. The structures of memory, narrative, and solidarity become the foundations for any critical theology. Such a theology is intentionally practical for it is determined by the categories of memory, narrative, and solidarity, this being the goal of Christian existence— solidarity with the living and the dead. Such a solidarity necessitates that theology be practical. Beyond this necessity to be practical, the very Christian idea of God is, according to Metz, "a practical idea. God cannot be thought of at all unless this idea irritates and encroaches on the immediate interests of the person who is trying to think of it. Thinking about God is a review of interests and needs that are directly related to ourselves."[35]

While Metz does not fully define what practical means, he does outline certain characteristics of praxis. Praxis must be ethical, i.e. concerned with right action both for society and for individuals. It must be historical, i.e. empirical in nature and therefore cannot be controlled by theory; it must also be pathetic, i.e. characterized by solidarity. An emphasis on the practical has clear epistemological implications. Truth and knowledge are understood primarily in terms of doing and transforming rather than in terms of contemplating. So praxis becomes for

Metz an essential category of Christian theology. Metz has emphasized the pathic nature of praxis: praxis is not simply action for, but also a being with, a compassion for the sufferer. It is solidarity in suffering not only with the living but also with the dead. For Metz, such an emphasis on the pathic aspect of praxis does not remove the Christian from the realm of political action. "On the contrary, it can only liberate praxis from its exclusive orientation towards an anthropological model, according to which man is viewed one-sidedly as a subject exerting control over nature and human history, the latter being regarded as a non-dialectical history of progress and triumph or conquest."[36]

Practical theology is for Metz political theology. Political for Metz is taken in a broad sense to mean that theology cannot escape history and society. Theology is political because its foundations lie in memory, narrative, and solidarity. If interdependence and solidarity characterize human existence, then theology will be political by nature; it will address itself to men and women in their holding environment which is society. The Christian faith as handed down through narratives and "dangerous memories" encounters people as social beings. There can be no privatization of the Christian faith.

Political theology will be essentially a narrative theology; as narrative, theology will encourage all Christians and others to be authentic story-tellers; it will be a theology that empowers Christians to become active subjects. Political theology must also be ecclesial. Here the church "must understand itself as the public witness and bearer of the tradition of a dangerous memory of freedom."[37]

Suffering and Eschatology

Metz's political theology, while emphasizing a discipleship that is transformative of situations of oppression, is also eschatological; while concerned with the "dangerous memories" of the past, and the present situations of oppression, theology has an orientation toward the future. The eschatological aspect of political theology is simply a reminder that all social institution and transformation are provisional and cannot be identified with the kingdom of God. Eschatology for Metz does not do away with responsibility for history. For Metz, eschatology simply implies that Christianity implies *disruption*.[38]

Eschatology for Metz implies that something radically new can occur in history.

What differentiates political theology done from a Christian perspective is Christianity's openness to suffering. Belief in technological progress or evolutionary processes proves to be illusory when the question of dealing with the emancipation of suffering arises. Usually within these theories the history of suffering is denied. Metz provides us with a basic understanding of eschatology: "The faith of Christians is a praxis in history and society that is to be understood as hope in solidarity in the God of Jesus as a God of the living and the dead who calls all men to be subjects in his presence."[39]

Christianity does not contain a theoretical explanation for innocent suffering; it offers the hopeful story and dangerous memory of the crucified Jesus. The story furnishes us with alternative visions of the world and offers us the possibility of imaging more creative ways of dealing with suffering. Christianity does not cover up the history of suffering but invites men and women to compassion: it keeps alive stories of suffering.

Conclusion

While Moltmann's emphasis is on the suffering God, Metz underlines the concreteness of the history of suffering. This history of suffering is interrupted by the failure of the cross and by the "dangerous memory" of this failure. There is a redemptive value to these narratives; yet what is most redemptive is the telling and the tellers of the story. There is a radical call to discipleship in Metz's political theology. Discipleship implies the role of tradition: the possibilities of discipleship for transformation lies in the power of the past and its openness for interpretation. Suffering as the point of departure of theology reveals the human subject as someone with a past and a future. As Metz points out, "What emerges from the memory of suffering is a knowledge of the future that does not point to empty anticipation, but looks actively for more human ways of life in the light of our experience of the new creation of man in Christ." Metz in his theology is in dialogue with those movements that seek the emancipation of suffering man/woman. Metz considers these movements as not offering the fullness of emancipation needed to truly deal with suffering, and often threatening society with various forms of totalitarianism. The suffering that is the object of emancipation cannot be reduced to socio-economic, political suffering. There is always the suffering of those who came before us, the history of suffering that is often neglected by emancipative movements. What seems to be lacking in Metz is an adequate theology of the God of Jesus Christ. As E. Schillebeeckx writes:

> Metz does not reflect on the concept of God as he is understood in the light of Jesus, as a God of pure positivity, as the author of good and enemy of evil. And this concept of God must colour what is in itself a correct theory of the narrative communication of the history of human suffering in a special way which Metz does not analyse.[40]

The most important criticism that can be directed at Metz's theology is that he emphasizes too radically nature over history, and that historical consciousness is alone the rubric for theological reflection. As a human subject, as a suffering subject, I belong to the world of nature as well as to the world of history. The split between history and nature ultimately affects one's understanding of salvation and therefore of suffering. The very nature of suffering does not justify a radical split between history and nature. The lack of harmony between men/women and their environment is clearly a source of great suffering.

5
Suffering from a Feminist Perspective: Dorothy Soelle

Introduction

One of the most provocative books written on theology and suffering in the past decade is that of Dorothy Soelle, and it is simply entitled *Suffering*.[1] Dorothy Soelle is a German theologian now residing in the United States. Her concern with suffering has much to do with personal and political issues. Growing up in the Germany of the 1930s, she was deeply marked by the holocaust and its implications for the Christian faith and for theology.

Faith and theology, in light of the holocaust, simply could no longer be perceived as having to do simply with suprahistorical realities, but had to be concerned with the realities of this world and this space. In her first book, Dorothy Soelle clearly affirmed that theology must be "a reflective description of certain experiences."[2] A theology that originates in experience cannot proceed deductively from well-established theological principles but inductively from human experiences.[3] "Theology begins with experience and sets experience over against the promise of a whole life, the promise of the Kingdom of God."[4] As human experiences, these occur within changing historical situations and are always personally conditioned and contextual. Dorothy Soelle's theology is marked by her own personal experiences and situations, from the holocaust, to the evils of capitalism, the genocide of Vietnam, and the ramifications of sexism. Throughout these various situations, the one connecting reality for Soelle is that of suffering, personal suffering and the suffering of others. Theology as a "reflective description of certain experiences," then, "originates in pain,"[5] and its "locus is suffering or the disregard for life that we experience all the time."[6] For Soelle "theology originates . . . in experiences of negative forces."[7] To a large extent, then, theology will be determined in its process and scope by the reality and nature of suffering.

Suffering and Powerlessness

Fundamental to the nature of suffering for Soelle is the experience of powerlessness. Powerlessness signifies "the expectancy or probability held by the individual that his own behavior cannot determine the occurrence of the outcomes, or reinforcements, he seeks."[8] Any attempt to change a situation of suffering must come to terms with a situation of powerlessness. Powerlessness is also accompanied by meaninglessness. Both of these elements bring about a situation of alienation. Suffering that alienates can be named affliction. Affliction is suffering that has at the same time physical, psychological, and social elements. It is the social element that is at the core of affliction. All of these characteristics of suffering will have implications for Soelle's understanding of theology. In fact, the reality of suffering leads her to combine different interests of theology such as feminism, liberation, and mysticism. For Soelle these different focuses of contemporary theology have a common denominator—involvement in the search for non-authoritarian human relationships and, therefore, opposition to suffering as affliction.

Feminist Theology and Liberation Theology

Feminist theology for Soelle is characterized by its opposition to powerlessness, a powerlessness "that religion glorifies and intensifies."[9] Feminist theology originates in pain and works toward the liberation from pain. Its greatest obstacles are an ideology of helplessness and a culture of apathy. The most important aspect of feminist theology lies in its attempt to reinterpret the concept of God. "The decisive change in our new understanding of liberation, of the women's movement, and of feminist theology is evident in our concept of God. The ways we address God, and the symbolism of God we use, change and have to change if we take this demand for liberation seriously and try to incorporate it into our lives."[10] The new understanding of God will have to do with categories of power and suffering, with the basic issue of theodicy. The basic thrust of feminist theology for Soelle must be directed by Christianity's conception "of God as a powerful, indeed as an all-powerful, father."[11] Dorothy Soelle cannot understand that after the reality of the holocaust, one can still talk about an almighty God. "It simply went beyond my powers to conceive of a powerful God who could look at Auschwitz, tolerate it, participate in it, observe it, or whatever. If he is all-powerful, then he is devoid of love. Such was my conclusion."[12]

This fundamental criticism led Soelle to a radical Christ-centered theology which emphasized solidarity with those who are powerless. For Soelle, "feminist theology grows out of an understanding of the God who is with the lowly, the disinherited and the offended and who speaks through them."[13]

Feminist theology will, because of its origin in suffering, be a liberation theology and emphasize a praxis-reflection-praxis process.[14] The only possible answer to suffering, the only viable goal to be attained, is "the abolition of circumstances under which people are forced to suffer."[15] Since the basic causes of suffering, understood as affliction, are social and cultural, a feminist theology will also be a critical political theology which "as reflection on faith must give attention to the social situation of those who are brutalized and uncover the social roots of their brutalization."[16] For Soelle, "Political theology is rather a theological hermeneutic, which in distinction from a theology that interprets reality from an ontological or existentialist point of view, holds open a horizon of interpretation in which politics is understood as the comprehensive and decisive sphere in which Christian truth should become praxis."[17] From the perspective of a political theology, liberation from suffering cannot be a solipsistic affair: it has to be social in nature and lead to social transformation. Again according to Soelle:

> A theology that understands itself apolitically will attempt to portray the gospel independently of this horizon of social transformations—which for us is indispensable. It

makes as a preliminary demand the surrender of social, political reason, which regards the world as transformable. A theology like Bultmann's will view history as having come to an end and will always interpret redemption as an escape from the world.[18]

Political theology as understood by Dorothy Soelle is a critical theology; it is one that does not sanction existing political and religious structures that oppress and cause suffering. It is a theology that is consistently aware of the social and political ramifications of all religious language.

From a feminist perspective, the basic question in theology is: "What does Christ mean for our human lives?"[19] And this question is connected to the achievement of personal identity. "How one can achieve personal identity" remains an essential question. But because individuals are essentially social beings, self-identity is always to some extent the product of a person's cultural context. To a large extent culture mediates self-understanding. The project of realizing an authentic self-identity must involve the critique of culture. In fact, for Dorothy Soelle, feminism today must bring about a new culture.

It is Dorothy Soelle's contention that one of the cultural elements that needs radical criticism is the individualism that permeates contemporary society. Within this situation there is no value given to the common good, and political life is effectively marginalized. The privatization of social and political life is also accompanied by a privatization of faith and of faith's relation to God, and even to the privatization of God.

The Culture of Apathy

The most negative aspect of this individualistic culture is apathy. Apathy is the inability to suffer. It affects people primarily in industrial nations and is a prime result of consumerism. A consumer culture is a pecuniary culture which involves an ethic, a standard of living and a power structure. To nurture and sustain itself, a consumer culture relies on important structural elements in advanced capitalist societies, such as the growing centralization of economic power among producers. A consumer culture is one where we are only as we possess and consequently are often possessed by our possessions.

Consumerism blinds the contented ones to the suffering present in their midst. Here apathy becomes "the no longer perceived numbness to suffering. Then the person and his circumstances are accepted as natural, which even on the technological level signifies nothing but blind worship of the status quo: no disruptions, no involvement, no sweat."[20]

Apathy is a form of the inability to feel pain. Socially, apathy is understood as a condition in which people are so dominated by the goal of avoiding suffering that such a goal leads to the avoidance of human relationships and contacts. Even expressions of physical pain are repressed. Physical pain is after all a sign of vitality and of the refusal simply to accept losses of functional disabilities. To desire freedom from pain means to desire death. The consequence of apathy is the desensitization that freedom from suffering involves, the inability to perceive reality.

In fact the attempt by our culture to dismiss the question of suffering is most destructive of our own humanness. "The ideal of a life free from suffering, the illusion of painlessness, destroys people's ability to feel anything."[21] In a state of apathy there can be no experience of joy so that life itself becomes flattened out.[22] "Apathy, an absence of suffering, and the desire to go through life without experiencing pain are all hallmarks of the culture dominant in the First World."[23] Apathy has a twofold dimension: "denial and repression of one's own suffering and icy indifference to the suffering of others."[24] Apathy is the opposite of love, love being the ability to be affected. For Dorothy Soelle, apathy and helplessness are the major obstacles to an authentic feminist theology, but they are not irreversible elements. The task of Christianity is to change and transform this situation.

Suffering and Language

The first step toward such a transformation has to do with the ability to find an adequate language to express suffering. The discovery of a language for suffering is the beginning of a change of the nature of suffering. The beginning of the transformation of suffering is linked to discovering a language which in itself presupposes the conviction that the world we live in can be changed. The phase of expression is the first step toward the elimination of suffering. Without the capacity to communicate with others, there can be no change.

The basic reason for the necessity of language is related to the nature of suffering as powerlessness. Every attempt at changing suffering must contend with powerlessness. The ability to speak about suffering is already a way of empowerment, and a way to deal with alienation.

Suffering that cannot be brought to language, to expression, is suffering that cannot be eliminated. Dorothy Soelle speaks of this suffering as mute suffering. Such a suffering "is senseless because the people affected by it no longer have any possibility of determining a course of action, of learning from their experience, or of taking measures that would change anything."[25] No theology can be developed to deal with such suffering for suffering, implies language about a situation.

The first step in conquering powerlessness is to find an appropriate language. A religious faith should provide such a language. Now the reasons for the role of language are that it fosters communication, and communication implies and even brings about solidarity. A mute suffering is basically like death; it is characterized by relationlessness.

> If people are not to remain unchanged in suffering, if they
> are not to be blind and deaf to the pain of others, if they are
> to move from purely passive endurance to suffering that
> can humanize them in a productive way, then one of the
> things they need is language.[26]

Without the ability to speak of one's suffering to others there is no hope of change. Now prayer is such a religious form of language that can address suffering. Prayer "is an act by which people dare to put their desires into words and thereby handle their suffering differently from the way society recommends to them."[27] Again "Prayer is an all-encompassing act by which people transcend the mute God of an apathetically endured reality and go over to the speaking God of a reality experienced with feeling in pain and happiness."[28]

There are two different reasons for the absence of language in a situation of suffering: one can be understood as mute suffering and the other as apathy. Mute suffering is a situation that cannot be reversed, while apathy can. Mute suffering is of such a kind that it reduces an individual to silence. It becomes a senseless form of suffering because the one who is suffering cannot change the situation and is basically reduced to passivity and submission. It is a form of suffering that leads to the abandonment of all hope. In such a situation death is perceived as truly attractive; suffering becomes the total focus and preoccupation of the individual.

The second reason for the absence of language is that of apathy. This is a reversible situation. Such a reversal becomes the main task of a feminist theology.

> My task as a theologian encompasses three operations: to translate whatever can be translated into modern scientific language; to eliminate anything that contradicts a commitment to love; to name, and stupidly (*blode*) to repeat, what I can neither translate nor put aside as superfluous.[29]

Suffering and God-Language

A basic function of theology is to enlarge our language about suffering. While there can be no "abstract" approach to suffering, yet there are universal lessons that can be learned from the individual suffering of the past and the present. According to Soelle "we cannot give up a language that transcends all that exists or is derivable only from what exists."[30] God-language is a language of universality and cannot be given up. So one of the first preoccupations of any feminist theology is God-language.

From Dorothy Soelle's theological perspective, the question of God-language is a moral issue deeply connected to our relationships. Social structures and ideologies permeate a society's language. Language is not merely an external feature of reality, but language is the main bearer and transmitter of the social structures. God-language relates to whole social structures and legitimizes given social orders. Her feminist approach to theology leads her to criticize traditional language and understanding of God and of theological interpretation of suffering, the two being closely related. Traditional theology conceives of God as all-powerful, "as an all-powerful father."[31] This symbol of God as all-powerful father has two components: one is power and the other is kindness. These two components make the symbol complex and dangerous. It is the claim of power and the type of power for God that is objected to by feminist theology. But Dorothy Soelle's questioning of the all-powerful God has its roots not simply in feminism, but also in the reality of Auschwitz.[32] Auschwitz led Dorothy Soelle to a more Christocentric theology basically in line with Bonhoeffer's own position. Christ is the one who died on the cross and what characterizes him is his non-authoritarian powerlessness. "His powerlessness constitutes his inner authority."[33]

Her experience of Auschwitz which led her to criticize Christianity's concept and symbol of God as all-powerful father also led her to criticize the traditional understanding of God's complete independence, expressed by the term *aseity*.[34] A theology that emphasizes relationship must necessarily be critical also of aseity. By such an "*a se*," God is isolated from the world and untouched by human suffering. Dorothy Soelle is critical of such an understanding.[35]

The God of Apathy

An apathetic God cannot lead us to an authentic understanding of suffering. For such a God "fulfills the ideal of one who is physically beyond the reach of external influences and psychologically anesthetized—like things that are dead . . . his apathy signifies his spirit's freedom from internal needs and external injuries."[36] Dorothy Soelle views the traditional Christian theology of suffering as a form of masochism involving a perversion of love. There is a constant tendency to contrast divine power with human powerlessness. "Affliction is regarded as human weakness that serves to demonstrate divine strength."[37] This can easily lead to accepting God as the cause of suffering, and the willingness on the part of the Christian to suffer. Such an attitude neglects to consider the various causes of suffering, and concentrates primarily in the acceptance and transformation of personal suffering and neglects the elimination of the other's suffering. "Suffering is there to break our pride, demonstrate our powerlessness, exploit our dependency. Affliction has the intention of bringing us back to a God who only becomes great when he makes us small."[38]

The worst aspect of such a sadistic understanding of suffering is the kind of theology of God that emerges from such an attitude, one that makes the wrath of God its essential aspect. Such an emphasis on the wrath of God also leads to an emphasis on human depravity.

The basic logic of such a sadistic understanding of suffering consists of three propositions: (1) God is the almighty ruler of the world, and sends all suffering; (2) God acts justly, not capriciously; (3) all suffering is punishment for sin.[39] Here the omnipotence of God is easily combined with justice but not so easily with love, and so the massive suffering of the innocent becomes problematic. Also problematic in the traditional Christian perspective is its apathetic concept of God. For Dorothy Soelle, the apathy of God has its roots in Greek philosophy.

> According to Aristotle one aspect of God's perfection is that he has no need for friends. This apathetic God became the God of the Christians, although he was a contradiction to the biblical God, with his emotions and suffering. The axiom that God was incapable of suffering became more and more acceptable.[40]

Although the scriptures are opposed to such a view, it is the Greek concept that won out in the long run so that even today "the theological question of whether God could suffer has not been settled."[41] The impassible God "is the almighty ruler whose only relationship with suffering is that he causes or sends it and that he takes it away."[42] While such an apathetic God is an obstacle to any attempt at giving meaning to suffering, it is truly a stumbling block, a "scandalon" when it comes to the suffering of the innocent.

God and the Suffering of the Innocent

While there is a suffering from which we can learn, there is a suffering that cannot be given a meaning and that is the suffering of the innocent. It is such suffering that leads to atheism. "Wherever people are confronted by senseless suffering, faith in a God who embodies both omnipotence and love has to waver or be destroyed."[43] Such innocent suffering goes against faith and trust in a loving God, so "atheism arises out of human suffering."[44] But this negation of God is not a negation of the God of Jesus but a theism "that has nothing to do with Christ."[45]

Innocent suffering poses the theodicy question most starkly and preempts any possibility of perceiving God as directly or indirectly involved with such innocent suffering. Dorothy Soelle is very severe toward the traditional position of theodicy.

> We have to guard against facile theological interpretations of suffering. From a Christian point of view, suffering does not exist in order to break our pride, demonstrate our impotence, or take advantage of our dependency. The purpose of suffering is not to lead us back to a God who attains to his greatness only by reducing us to insignificance.[46]

It can never be affirmed that God can cause suffering in any way. On this point Dorothy Soelle is quite critical of Jürgen Moltmann's position. She perceives Moltmann as affirming that God the Father is the author of Jesus' suffering, the omnipotent Father who delivers the Son to suffering.[47] For Soelle, Moltmann's position remains problematic. It cannot resolve the tension between the loving God of the incarnation, the one in solidarity with us, and the wrathful God of the cross. For Soelle Jesus simply cannot have suffered because of God. For Soelle the cross is not the symbol of the relation of the Father to the Son, but of Jesus to the world. The cross is above all a symbol of reality: love that confronts oppressive structures usually ends on a cross. Love does not cause suffering or produce it, although it must necessarily seek confrontation.

Dorothy Soelle's criticism of the apathetic God-Father led her to a greater emphasis on the person of Jesus Christ.

> The son was closer to me than the father, he revealed what the father could not communicate to me: love without privileges; love which empties itself and takes on the shape of a slave, a proletarian love which prefers to go to hell as long as others are condemned to stay there.[48]

For Soelle our only way to God is through Jesus: God can only be experienced in the powerlessness of Jesus Christ.[49] In the gospels, Jesus as the human face of God is truly the powerless one, the man for others. He is the one who refused to come down from the cross. "The only capital with which he came into the world was his love, and it was as powerless and as powerful as love is."[50] In a very frank description of her own evolution, Soelle writes the following:

> I had left behind belief in an omnipotent father "who rules all things so gloriously," derived from theism. For me, the metaphor of the "death of God" meant deliberately giving up the notion of the omnipotence of God as theologically and ethically impossible. In the light of Auschwitz the assumption of the omnipotence of God seemed—and still seems!—to me to be a heresy, a misunderstanding of what God means. From this criticism of the theistic-patriarchal God I developed a position in which the cross of Christ stands in the centre, as an affirmation of the non-violent impotence of love in which God himself is no longer one who imposes suffering, but a fellow sufferer.[51]

The God of Jesus is the "Abba," not the omnipotent Father who ordains the suffering of Jesus; this God is a loving God who does not avoid the suffering connected to such love. The God of Jesus Christ is a compassionate God who has the ability to feel the other's pain.

The Cross and Power

To approach God from our experience of the powerlessness of Jesus is to reinterpret the relationship between transcendence and immanence as one which cannot be thought of in hierarchical terms. "God's transcendence, often complained about as being his male side, was always still higher, more true, more authentic than his immanence, which nowadays is being reclaimed by feminist theology."[52] In light of Jesus Christ, God has truly made himself available. As Soelle writes, "the compassionate man from Samaria finds God and is found by God on the road. So, too, the truth/love/beauty of God can shine forth in our everyday life."[53] The God of Jesus Christ implies radical immanence and "means that God hallows our everyday life, that God is 'in' our this-worldliness if we have not destroyed our commitment through 'hatred'—disguised as normality and indifference."[54]

Does the radical immanence of God signify that God has abandoned all power? Besides the mystery of the cross there is also the mystery of the resurrection. For Soelle the resurrection is a form of power, but of good power. The resurrection is "the victory of life over death, of love over apathy."[55] The power of the resurrection is the power of solidarity.[56] The God of Jesus is a God who invites participation and exchange and challenges the absoluteness attributed to God. This change in the concept of the power of God is an essential element in a feminist theology.

> We cease to project God as the omnipotent one over against whom we then stand in total helplessness, and thus also change the relationship of this world to the other world or, to use another geometrical picture, of the horizontal and vertical.[57]

What this concept of power emphasizes is not submission but solidarity, not obedience but freedom. These two elements—solidarity and freedom—are reflected in Jesus' suffering. Jesus' suffering was not dictated by God; it was avoidable, yet Jesus endured it freely and went to Jerusalem and confronted the powers. Jesus' "Suffering freely borne has a cleansing, reconciling, saving power."[58] To the suffering of Jesus and that of the Christian, there are two elements: freedom and solidarity. Suffering is "given to God, it benefits everyone. You do not suffer for yourself alone, or for the pedagogical ends of your self-realization..." Christian discipleship, as a form of solidarity, connects personal and political pain with the pain of God.

> Our own pain, which we have accepted, will then be related to the pains of the people among whom we live. We stop hoping for a solution from without. . . To "serve the pain of God by your own pain" is to lead suffering out of its private little corner and to achieve human solidarity.[60]

The imitator of Christ which every faithful person is exhorted to be can choose to endure suffering because of the conviction that through pain another will escape pain. The disciples' role is to suffer in the place of others, as Jesus suffered for us all. So a feminist approach such as Dorothy Soelle's must ask questions such as: Do we need the death of God, of Jesus to show us that God is with us in our suffering? Was God not with us in our suffering before the death of Jesus? Did the death really initiate something that did not exist before? Is it right to see the death of Jesus as a symbol for the life—giving power of receptivity to reality? Much of the feminist approach is challenging the traditional understanding of atonement especially as it relates to an interpretation of suffering.

The Uniqueness of Jesus' Suffering

Dorothy Soelle is critical of the traditional understanding of the uniqueness of Jesus' suffering and death. For her neither God's abandonment nor the nature of Jesus' suffering makes them different from those of other men and women. The reality of suffering for everyone including Jesus is powerlessness.

This becomes clear in the Gethsemane narrative.[61] For Dorothy Soelle, the truth of the symbol of the Cross must be found in the repeatability of Jesus' suffering. This is also an important feminist position.

> Wherever a person is conscious of dying, wherever pain is experienced, there too one's earlier certainty about God is destroyed. People have given testimonies that demonstrate that the symbol can be repeated, that is, that it can be appropriated. They have experienced Gethsemane, the fear of death, but also the conquest of all fears in the place in which the cup of suffering is drunk to the bitter dregs.[62]

While Dorothy Soelle challenges the understanding of the role of Jesus' suffering in our atonement, this does imply that the cross is not the center of her theology. The cross remains the symbol of love that refuses to betray its very nature: its concern for the welfare of the other. First comes love, then comes suffering. The cross is the symbol of God's compassionate love. A compassionate love finds its way to the cross. Compassion somehow constrains us to suffer with the other; it demands solidarity with the other.

A Mystical Approach to Suffering

It is the compassionate nature of love that leads Soelle to a mystical understanding of suffering. Compassion enables one to be centered on the other; there is a for-otherness central to compassion. As Soelle writes:

> It is the mystic sufferer who open his hands for everything coming his way. He has given up faith and hope for a God who reached into the world from the outside, but not hope for changing suffering and learning from suffering.[63]

A mystical approach to reality implies a yes to life and to reality in all of its form; mysticism is the opposite of repression in all of its forms. A true acceptance of reality implies a deeper love for reality, a love that avoids placing conditions on reality. The acceptance of suffering is part of the great "yes" to life as a whole. To be able to believe means to say "yes" to this life, to this finitude, to work on it and hold it open for the promised future. With Paul Tillich, Soelle concurs that a true acceptance of reality implies a deeper love for reality: a love that avoids placing conditions on reality. What makes Soelle's assent to suffering possible is concentration on a greater cause. Acceptance is not toleration. The acceptance of suffering is part of the great "yes" to life as a whole. Christianity demands "that one accept suffering with courage as an element of finitude and affirm finitude in spite of the suffering that accompanies it."[64] Suffering can bring us to the point of wishing that the world did not exist; of believing that non-being is better than being. It can bring us to despair and destroy our capacity for affirmation. The truth about life lies in acceptance. "Every acceptance of suffering is an acceptance of that which exists."[65]

The denial of every form of suffering can result in a flight from reality in which contact with reality becomes ever thinner. Such an acceptance of reality can supersede theodicy. "The theodicy question is superseded by an unlimited love for reality. In this context God is no answer, "plays no role at all.... God is the symbol for our unending capacity to love. Here the basic attitude is love toward God—toward one who certainly is not over us like a perfect being—but one who is in the process of becoming—as is everything we love."[66] This love, as

all love, is without conditions; it cannot be made dependent on the fulfillment of certain conditions. Love of God can be stronger than every
form of affliction, in a way stronger than God. "Mystical theology
answers suffering with a love in view of which the 'Lord' has to feel
ashamed for it is stronger than he—no longer God as Lord. Such
unconditional love transcends every God who is less than *love*."[67]

Christianity does make a very strong affirmation of suffering, at
times almost in a sadistic way. It does so because clearly at the center
of Christianity lies the paschal mystery. This affirmation of suffering
must be accompanied by the acceptance of life.

> In a certain sense learning presupposes mystical accep-
> tance: the acceptance of life, an indestructible hope. The
> mystics have described how a person could become free
> and open, so that God is born within the depths of his soul;
> they have pointed out that a person in suffering can
> become "calm" rather than apathetic, and that the capacity
> for love is strongest where it grows out of suffering.[68]

This mystical approach to suffering is connected to Dorothy
Soelle's teaching on the role of Jesus' humanity. For Soelle the suffering of the poor and of the people is connected to the suffering of Jesus.
As she writes, "the time of the passion is the present."[69] Again, "really
living like Christ will not mean reward, social recognition and an
assured income, but difficulties, discrimination, solitude, anxiety."[70]
"The message of Jesus is that the more you grow in love the more vulnerable you make yourself."[71]

Conclusion

In establishing her feminist approach to theology, Dorothy Soelle
has demonstrated how one's approach to suffering has clear connec-
tions to one's understanding of God and vice versa. Her criticism of
the traditional understanding of suffering leads her to a reevaluation of
the nature of God's immanence viewed in light of the paschal mystery.
She perceives God as a fellow sufferer, a partner in the process of cre-

ation, a co-creator. While the powerlessness of God is made abundant-ly clear, God's power as revealed in the mystery of the resurrection is not as evident. And therefore the eschatological transformative value of human solidarity with God in suffering and creating remains ulti-mately without clear foundations.

6
Liberation Theology and Suffering: The Theology of Gustavo Gutierrez

Introduction

Many theologians today affirm that the voices of those who suffer must be heard. Suffering in its various forms has always been a basic question for most religions and their theologies. Of the many theologies that take suffering seriously, none does more so than liberation theology. Liberation theology has accepted as its task the articulation of the pain of the world. From its very beginning, liberation theology has argued that in the doing of theology, context is especially important, for context determines the way theology will be done, and how content will be organized. A theology that sees itself as contextual will give critical attention to the relationship of theological ideas to the particular situation of the theologian. There can be different contexts— geographical, economic, social; for liberation, the fundamental context "must be that of historical reality."[1] According to liberation theology this historical reality is marked by suffering. For Jon Sobrino the "task of theology is to find its place in the reality of this suffering world, to find a place within the very suffering of this world."[2] Again, the author affirms that "the place of theology is the suffering of the world, and to stand in its place means to stand within the actual suffering that racks this world."[3] Of all the different worlds that men and women inhabit, the "hardest" is the world of suffering. Sobrino perceives liberation theology as "a theology historically necessary in a suffering world and systematically adequate for giving an account of Christian faith in a suffering world."[4] Essential to liberation theology is the way it perceives suffering and the causes of suffering. Again, according to Sobrino, "for liberation theology, the major form of suffering in today's world is historical suffering—suffering unjustly inflicted on some by others."[5] Historical suffering is understood as massive suffering "affecting the majority of humanity making it practically impossible for people to direct their own lives...."[6] A further and more specific thesis of liberation theology concerns the cause of such suffering. According to Sobrino: "On the human-natural level, the greatest cause of massive, cruel, and intolerable suffering in today's world is the poverty found in the Third and the Fourth World."[7] Poverty is the fundamental cause of suffering in the world, and it is also the basic form of suffering. Poverty leads to the destruction of humanness itself and to the abolition of solidarity itself. For Sobrino, poverty "insofar as it is rooted in injustice stands forth as the greatest of moral evils and expresses the fundamental sin of this world—the destruction of life."[8] Poverty is the main reason why the theodicy question remains a basic question. For liberation theology, poverty is the *analogatum princeps* of all suffering. Poverty as experienced in the third world is analogous and most representative of the suffering that appears at paradigmatic moments of the history of salvation—Moses and the exodus; the prophets and the exile; Jesus and the cross.

There is a specific cause to the massive poverty and suffering in the third world and also in other worlds. According to Sobrino, "from a historical perspective, the causes of sufferings in the Third World are to a great extent to be found in the First World."[9] The cause of poverty and suffering in the world lies in oppressive structures of the first world.

Theology is contextualized by massive historical suffering, and its fundamental purpose is the elimination of suffering. Sobrino writes: "If a theology closes its eyes to suffering because such suffering is not occurring massively in 'its' world . . . that theology would disassociate itself from the real historical humanity in which we all live and which, theologically, is God's own creation."[10] The elimination of suffering is not only the task of theology but such an elimination "carries on divine revelation."[11] To eliminate poverty and suffering is to promote the kingdom of God. "The end purpose of theology is to clarify and facilitate how humanity is to respond and correspond to God within history."[12]

Such a theology must be characterized by praxis and marked by compassion: "Before a world of suffering, the primary response must be a compassion that seeks to eliminate such suffering...."[13] Compassion characterizes God's relation to humanity and Jesus' ministry to the oppressed and the sick. Praxis is an essential element of compassion, for the primary purpose of compassion is the liberation from poverty and suffering. "What remains fundamentally clear is that the end purpose of liberation theology is the liberation of the suffering world."[14]

Suffering and Poverty

Suffering has many faces and many causes. A theology that is concerned with suffering will necessarily be determined to a large extent by the kind of suffering it is addressing. Liberation theology in its many various forms is a theology that formally addresses the question of suffering caused by injustice. By emphasizing the subject of suffering, the poor, we can hope to understand adequately the present reality of human existence. For liberation theology, God is known in the midst of suffering; liberation theology seeks to speak about God in the situation of suffering. Yet liberation theology takes a different direction from that of other contemporary theologies concerned with suffering. The focus of liberation theology is the situation of massive public suffering, the suffering of the poor masses, especially those in Latin America. The suffering of the poor is a specific kind of suffering with specific causes. The poor are the economically disadvantaged, and because of such a deprivation the poor suffer powerlessness and oppression. Peter Henriot writes that "to be poor is to be hungry, to be without decent shelter and clothes, to lack adequate educational and health care opportunities, to be unemployed, to be on the margin of society, to feel excluded from decisions that affect you, to feel controlled by outside forces, to be unable to deal with problems of daily existence, to be discriminated against."[15]

That suffering is the fundamental theme of liberation theology is made evident in the following words of Bishop Desmond Tutu:

> Liberation theology more than any other kind of theology
> issues out of the crucible of human suffering and anguish.
> It happens because people cry out, "Oh, God, how long?"
> "Oh, God, but why?" All liberation theology stems from
> trying to make sense of human suffering when those who
> suffer are the victims of organized oppression and
> exploitation, when they are emasculated and treated as less
> than what they are: human persons created in the image of
> the Triune God, redeemed by the one Savior Jesus Christ
> and sanctified by the Holy Paraclete. This is the genesis of
> all liberation theology and so also of black theology, which
> is theology of liberation in Africa.[16]

These words were quoted by Gustavo Gutierrez in the introduction of his most important work on suffering: *On Job, God-Talk and
the Suffering of the Innocent.*[17]

Poverty and the Task of Theology

Gustavo Gutierrez is a Peruvian priest and theologian who
knows the meaning of suffering from inside. As a child he experienced
the suffering of a disease that has left him lame. But deeper and more
cutting was his experience of poverty and struggle by which most
Peruvians are marked. This complex experience of suffering is a pervasive theme in Gutierrez's works. Gutierrez does his theology from the
perspective of those who suffered. "Human suffering, involvement
with it, and the questions it raises about God are in fact one point of
departure and one central theme in the theology of liberation."[18] The
basic task of theology becomes: How are we to talk about a God who
is revealed as love in a situation characterized by poverty and oppression? How are we to proclaim the God of life to men and women who
die prematurely and unjustly? How are we to acknowledge that God
makes us a free gift of love and justice when we have before us the
suffering of the innocent? What words are we to use in telling those
who are not even regarded as persons that they are the daughters and
sons of God? These are key questions being asked in the theology that

has been forming in Latin America and in other places throughout the world where the situation is the same.[19] For Gutierrez more than for any other Latin American liberation theologian, suffering is the basic question for theology.

Gutierrez's theology moves in two distinguishable stages that are characterized by two different theological emphases. The first stage is marked by an emphasis on poverty as the cause of suffering. In this stage the basic biblical symbol is that of the exodus and the emphasis is on liberating praxis. The basic purpose of theology is the liberating of the poor from their poverty and therefore from their suffering. The second stage is brought about by a deeper reflection on the nature of suffering, especially its irrefractability. Here the emphasis on the liberating praxis is replaced by an emphasis on the gratuitous love of God. Here the biblical symbol is that of the exile, and the language about God is more of the contemplative type than that of the prophetic type. From the perspective of the intractability of suffering, Gutierrez sees the love and presence and fidelity of God as an overwhelming reality.

The Many Faces of Poverty

In both stages, the one unifying factor is the presence of the poor. For Gutierrez the poor "irrupt" in our history.[20] The "irruption" of the poor on the historical scene is a revelation of a contrast situation, a disclosure of contradiction that ruptures history itself. Yet in the midst of this contrast, at the very center of this rupture God is being experienced in a new way. For "in the midst of many and varied forms of suffering something new is being born in Latin America. This is what prompts talk of a *kairos*, a favorable time, a moment when the Lord knocks on the doors of the ecclesial community that lives in Latin America and asks it to open so that he may come and dine there (Rev. 3:20)."[21]

Poverty has many forms and faces. There is *material poverty*, "that is, the lack of economic goods necessary for a human life worthy of the name. In this sense poverty is considered degrading and is rejected by the conscience of contemporary persons."[22] The Christian tradition often speaks about *spiritual poverty* "as an interior attitude of detachment from the goods of this world."[23] While this understanding flies at the roots of much Christian spirituality, it can in the long run lead "to comforting and tranquilizing conclusions."[24] Here the possession of material goods can be accompanied by a spirit of detachment. The lack of material goods does not seem to be of major concern for those who emphasize this understanding. According to Gutierrez, there is also a biblical understanding of poverty. "In the Bible poverty is a scandalous condition inimical to human dignity and therefore contrary to the will of God."[25] This kind of poverty has to be opposed and condemned: Such "poverty is an expression of a sin, that is, of a negation of love. It is therefore incompatible with the coming of the kingdom of God, a kingdom of love and justice."[26] Since such poverty is an evil, "to eliminate it is to bring closer the moment of seeing God face to face, in union with other persons."[27]

The Bible also sees poverty as *spiritual childhood*, as the ability to welcome God. "This poverty has no direct relationship to wealth; in the first instance it is not a question of indifference to the goods of this world. It goes deeper than that; it means to have no other sustenance than the will of God."[28] This poverty is the fundamental attitude of Christ. "For you know how generous our Lord Jesus Christ has been: he was rich, yet for our sake became poor, so that through his poverty you might become rich" (2 Cor 8:9). Such voluntary poverty is an act of redemptive love, for it is "a commitment of solidarity with the poor, with those who suffer misery and injustice."[29] Such poverty as Christian poverty "is an expression of love, is solidarity with the poor and is a protest *against poverty*."[30] The poor of today are the materially poor, "the oppressed one, the one marginalized from society, the member of the proletariat struggling for the most basic right...."[31]

Gutierrez believes that material poverty has specific causes: it is most often the consequence of distorted social and personal values. The distance between the poor countries and the rich ones in our capitalist world is widening, as numerous studies by international agencies have shown. The upsurge of capitalism and the situation of the poor in recent decades have demonstrated once again that capitalist development is of its very nature detrimental to the masses. The naked exploitation now endured by the poor nations of the world all too abundantly attests to this.[32]

Poverty and Injustice

Poverty caused by oppressive social, political, and economic structures is the cause of a specific kind of suffering, the unmerited suffering of the innocent. "Here the masses of the poor suffer an inhuman situation that is evidently undeserved. Nothing can justify a situation in which human beings lack the basic necessities for a life of dignity and in which their most elementary rights are not respected. The suffering and the destructive effect on individuals go far beyond what is seen in a first contact with the world of the poor."[33] The focusing point of liberation theology is the suffering subject, the innocent, oppressed, and victimized subject.

The suffering of the poor is the suffering of the dispossessed; it has the non-identity character of a non-person. The suffering of the poor challenges all illusions about progress and security. So for Gustavo Gutierrez "the suffering of the innocent and the questions it leads them to ask are indeed problems for theology, that is, for discourse about God."[34]

Gutierrez's theology attempts to meet this challenge. The "irruption" of the poor challenges theology to contribute to their liberation and therefore to alleviate their suffering. But the existence of the poor is not a fated fact; it is not neutral on the political level or innocent of ethical implications. Poor people are by-products of the system under which we live and for which we are responsible. Poor people are the ones who have been shunted to the sidelines of our socio-cultural world. Poor people are those who are oppressed and exploited, who are deprived of the fruits of their labor and stripped of their life and reality as human beings. Poor people are members of the proletarian class. That is why the poverty of the poor is not a summons to alleviate their plight with acts of generosity but rather a compelling obligation to fashion an entirely different social order.[35]

The Fundamental Option for the Poor

According to Gutierrez, God has chosen to reveal himself in the poor. Such a revelation demands the response of faith. This response is characterized by a fundamental option for the poor and for the identification of the Christian faith as a journey of liberating solidarity. For

Gutierrez the option for the poor is a way for Christianity to be truly universal. He indicates that "solidarity with the poor, with their struggles and their hopes, is the condition of an authentic solidarity with everyone—the condition of a universal love that makes no attempt to gloss over the social oppositions that obtain in the concrete history of peoples, but strides straight through the middle of them to a kingdom of justice and love."[36] For Gutierrez, faith must lead to deeds and action. The God who liberates in history, the Christ made poor, can only be preached with works, with gestures in a practice of solidarity with the poor.[37]

Liberation and Language

Theology can then be defined only within the context of liberation.[38] The task of theology is that of speaking correctly about God amid unjust suffering, and "this is especially true of situations in which the suffering reaches massive proportions."[39] Again "our task here is to find the words with which to talk about God in the midst of the starvation of millions, the humiliation of races regarded as inferior, discrimination against women, especially women who are poor, systematic social injustice, a persistently high rate of infant mortality, those who simply 'disappear' or are deprived of their freedom, the sufferings of peoples who are struggling for their right to live, the exiles and the refugees, terrorism of every kind, and the corpse-filled common graves of Ayacucho. What we must deal with is not the past but, unfortunately, a cruel present and a dark tunnel with no apparent end."[40]

Yet such language about God demands solidarity with those who suffer; first comes presence to the poor, and, then, language. "Only if we know how to be silent and involve ourselves in the suffering of the poor will we be able to speak out of their hope. Only if we take seriously the suffering of the innocent and live the mystery of the cross amid that suffering, but in the light of Easter, can we prevent our theology from being 'windy arguments' (Job 16:3). But if we do, then we shall not deserve to hear from the poor the reproach that Job threw in the faces of his friends: "What sorry comforters you are! (16:2)."[41]

Yet in the face of massive unmerited suffering there is a need to speak. How are human beings to find a language applicable to God in the midst of innocent suffering? This question, with all its implications for our understanding of the justice and unmerited generosity of God, is the great theme of the book of Job. Job stubbornly insists on his innocence. How, then, is a human being to speak of God and to God in the situation that Job must endure?[42] In order to address the situation of innocent suffering the language about God must be both prophetic and contemplative.

Suffering and Prophetic Language

"Two types of language thus emerge as the two closest approximations to a correct language about God: the language of prophecy and the language of contemplation."[43] Since one cannot truly speak about suffering without being committed to the poor, such a commitment demands a prophetic language. Prophetic language is basically a language of protest. "Those who suffer unjustly have a right to complain and protest."[44] The protest is against the situation and even against God. As prophetic language, it often begins in a personal experience, but it does not remain a private language. It extends to other situations of innocent suffering, to the needs of others. While prophetic language is one of protest, even protest against God, it is also a statement about what God must be like. The prophetic language is deeply ethical. It emphasizes the "oughtness" not only of the situation but also of God: God himself must be committed to the innocent suffering. God cannot be God and accept the situation of suffering.

Such a prophetic stance is taken by Jesus. Jesus is the model and symbol of opposition to poverty and suffering. The salvation brought about by Jesus embraces the whole of reality and implies an opposition to whatever is an obstacle to full humanity. Jesus liberates us from the very root of social injustice and brings to completion the entire dynamism of human history. The kingdom of God preached by Jesus functions in a subversive way, for it appeals for equality and justice for all.

In his liberative and prophetic actions, Jesus is a revelation and symbol of God, the compassionate God. God is a God who saves us not through his domination but through his suffering. Here we have Bonhoeffer's famous thesis of God's *weakness*: "It is of this God, and only of this God, that the Bible tells us. And it is thus that the cross acquires its tremendous revelatory potential with respect to God's

weakness as an expression of his love for a world come of age."[45]
While the cross reveals God's solidarity with those who suffer, the resurrection reveals the power of solidarity.

While Gustavo Gutierrez is much influenced by the Old
Testament, his theology is fundamentally christological. "The key to
every theological interpretation is Christ, and it was precisely the
coherence of Christ's word with his practice that led him to his death.
A christological approach makes it possible to subsume the experiences of, and reflections on, the faith that the poor have realized
throughout the course of history, and incorporate these experiences and
reflections into a valid and authentic theology. At the same time a
christological perspective will open for us the future of the resurrection, the life that conquers death, and that we know we have within us
'because we love our brothers and sisters' (cf. 1 John 3:14)."[46] The salvation that is brought about by God in Christ's death and resurrection
must be one that liberates from sin and its consequences, such as injustice and oppression. "Liberation is another word for salvation.
Liberation is living out one's salvation in the concrete historical conditions of today. Theology of liberation is not a theology of political liberation, although political liberation is one aspect of salvation.[47] Since
the basic roots of poverty and suffering are social, political, and economic, salvation in Christ must be spoken in a social sense.

A prophetic understanding of the Christian reality is also accomplished by a specific anthropology. "From a cosmological vision, man
moves to an anthropological vision . . . Man perceives himself as a creative subject. Moreover, man becomes aware . . . that he is an agent of
history, responsible for his own destiny. His mind discovers not only
the laws of nature, but also penetrates those of society, history, and
psychology. This new self-understanding of man necessarily brings in
its wake a different way of conceiving his relationship with God."[48]

While the kingdom of God simply cannot be equated with a new
political, social, and economic order, they are not unconnected. "The
Gospel does not provide a utopia for us, this is a human work. The
Word is a free gift of the Lord. But the Gospel is not alien to the historical plan; on the contrary, the human plan and the gift of God imply
each other. The Word is the foundation and meaning of all human
experience, this foundation is attested to and this meaning is con-
cretized through human actions."[49] For Gutierrez men and women who

struggle for the coming of the kingdom must live constantly out of hope. Hope transforms the reality of their world.[50] Such a hope, while future oriented, utopian in essence, not only announces a new reality but also denounces the present reality. "Utopia necessarily means a denunciation of the existing order. Its deficiencies are to a large extent the reason for the emergence of a utopia. The repudiation of a dehumanizing situation is an unavoidable aspect of utopia. It is a matter of a complete rejection which attempts to strike at the roots of the evil. This is why utopia is revolutionary and not reformist."[51]

In its prophetic stage, theology is perceived by Gutierrez as a rhetorical practice of liberating transformation. What comes first in this theology is the recommitment to the poor. Liberation theology has maintained that active commitment to liberation comes first and theology develops from it. Liberation theology reflects on and from within the complex and fruitful relationship between theory and practice.

In this theology praxis precedes reflection, and the subject of that praxis is the poor. This aspect of praxis is well expressed by José Comblin.

> Only the poor are able to feel what salvation, hope, justice, and justification are; only those who have felt throughout their lives, and are presently feeling what suffering, oppression, and injustice mean are able to hear God's promise and God's liberation. Only the person who has been rejected is able to understand what God's mercy means. In this sense, the experience of the poor is the starting point of a true knowledge of Christianity.[52]

Suffering and Contemplative Language

While the prophetic approach to the Christian reality and to the mystery of suffering is an essential element of Gutierrez's theology, it is considered insufficient. The basic reason for this, as already mentioned, is the nature of suffering. "But this kind of talk about God— talk that may be described as 'prophetic'—is inadequate. Job's thirst for understanding, which his trials have awakened and inflamed, is not satisfied. Gropingly, and resisting false images, he looks insatiably for a deeper insight into divine justice and an unlimited encounter with the

God in whom he believes and hopes."[53] Besides prophetic language, contemplative language is necessary. The basis of the language of contemplation is an encounter with a personal God characterized by freedom and gracious love. This gracious love Gutierrez sees as present to the suffering of the poor. They are the true subjects of history not out of any inevitable force, but out of God's free choice. God has opted for the poor and the suffering.

At the level of contemplation it is not only the justice of God that must be considered when we deal with suffering. "Only when we have come to realize that God's love is freely bestowed do we enter fully and definitively into the presence of the God of faith. Grace is not opposed to the quest for justice, nor does it play it down; on the contrary, it gives it its full meaning. God's love, like all true love, operates in a world not of cause and effect but of freedom and gratuitousness. That is how persons successfully encounter one another in a complete and unconditional way, without payment of any kind of charges and without externally imposed obligations that pressure them into meeting the expectations of the other."[54] In moving into a contemplative approach to suffering, it is not a question of forgetting about the demands of justice, but of positing those demands within the context of God's gratuitous love. "Nothing, no human work however valuable, merits grace, for if it did, grace would cease to be grace."[55] God is always and everywhere transcendent, and his love flows always graciously. "God is entirely independent of space and time. God acts only in accordance with the utterly free divine will: God does what God pleases to do. No love at all can be locked in."[56] Both prophetic and contemplative languages are necessary to speak about God in the context of innocent suffering, and both languages tell us something different about suffering. "Belief in God and God's gratuitous love leads to a preferential option for the poor and to solidarity with those who suffer wretched conditions, contempt, and oppression, those whom the social order ignores and exploits. The God of utter freedom and gratuitousness who has been revealed to Job can alone explain the privileged place of those whom the powerful and the self-righteous of society treat unjustly and make outcasts. In the God of Christian revelation, gratuitousness and preferential love for the poor go hand in hand. They are therefore also inseparable in our contemplation of God and our concern for the disinherited of this world."[57]

The language of contemplation in no way erodes the prophetic will to protest and to action but it prevents the distortion that turns these values into fruitless resignation and passivity in the face of injustice. There are times that in the face of overwhelming suffering only silence is possible.[58] Both approaches to suffering are necessary and not superfluous.[59]

Gutierrez preserves, even in his emphasis on liberating praxis, the mystery of God and ultimately the mystery of suffering. Prophecy and contemplation are journeys that are endless.[60] So theology must proceed from within the full paschal mystery; it moves from the experience of the cross to the joy of the resurrection and life. The theology that addresses innocent suffering must be made up of silence, contemplation, practice, of speech enriched by silence.

Liberation and Spirituality

So at the roots of Gutierrez's theology of liberation we find a spirituality. Spirituality here means that we have to move beyond the justice of God to the gracious love of God. Spirituality implies that the demands of justice not be forgotten. Spirituality is an emphasis on the authentic transcendence of God's freedom and love. So an authentic spirituality does imply a retreat from the world. An authentic and profound sense of God does not preclude awareness of the poor and the questions they raise. "Spirituality" does not preclude "social conscience." The real incompatibility is between bourgeois individualism and spirituality. The Christian spirituality has its foundation in both in the exodus and the exile: it is completely paschal in nature. Liberation theology moves from the experience of the cross to the joy of the resurrection and life.

So at the roots of the theology of liberation we find a spirituality, a mysticism. For Gutierrez this spirituality, while clearly centered in God, also has very deep christological roots. According to Gutierrez biblical faith is faith in a God who reveres himself as savior in historical events, and the exodus is the prime example of such historical activity. While the exodus discloses God as a God of and for the people, such a liberating immanence of God is fully realized in the person of Jesus. Here the cross becomes the central event revealing the depth of God's solidarity with those who suffer. Gutierrez compares Jesus to

Job, Job having anticipated Jesus' own witnessing to suffering. "Jesus speaks to us of the Father, and in his discourses, language about God achieves its greatest expressiveness. The Son of God teaches us that talk of God must be mediated by the experience of the cross. He accepts abandonment and death precisely in order to reveal God to us as love."[61] What Jesus experienced on the cross is the suffering of the innocent and the basic abandonment of such a suffering, especially the abandonment of God. According to Gutierrez, "This radical communion with the suffering of human beings brought him down to the deepest level of history at the very moment when his life was ending."[62] Yet on the cross Jesus also expresses his hope in a liberating hope, a hope that comes to fruition in the resurrection. "His cry on the cross renders more audible and more penetrating the cries of all the Jobs, individuals and collective, of human history. To adopt a comparison that Bonhoeffer uses in another context, the cry of Jesus is the *Cantus Firmus.* The leading voice to which all the voices of those who suffer unjustly are joined."[63]

So the option for the poor, the option for those who suffer, necessitates a spirituality, a mystical and political spirituality.[64] In opting for the poor we are opting for that which is deepest in God and in us—God's spirit, God's love.

Conclusion

Latin American liberation theology as so fully represented by Gustavo Gutierrez is a new interpretation of the basic meaning of the paschal mystery, combining theology, spirituality, and liberating solidarity. The intent of this solidarity is to deliver the poor from their oppression and, therefore, from their suffering. Such a solidarity is an "already presence of eschatological salvation."

The redemptive nature of the incarnation lies in the fact that in Christ God has established God's solidarity with those who suffer and through Christ, as the incarnation of God, Christian discipleship becomes a way in which the kingdom comes to expression.

Liberation theology, in its various forms and different phases, dialogues with those who, because of their suffering, experience meaninglessness. For liberation theology the true knowledge of God is not only discerned on the cross of Jesus Christ, but on the many contemporary crosses of the poor and the oppressed. Liberation theology is seeking to speak about God for those who suffer and very often have no voice. To speak about God for liberation theologians is not simply to add a new *logos* about a traditional *theos*, but it involves the bringing of speech to action. It is a theology that emphasizes God's liberating activity and Christian ecclesial praxis. Theology taken in its most formal sense will have to concern itself with questions of justice, of salvation as liberation, with political, social, and economic structures in actual situations of oppressive suffering. In fact, Latin American liberation theology is governed by its option for the poor. The poor here are the economically disadvantaged, the materially deprived, and thus suffer powerlessness, exploitation and oppression. Liberation theology in all of its various forms is connected by the reality of suffering, and while there is a common nature to suffering, liberation theology addresses the question of massive public suffering. For liberation theology, God is experienced in solidarity with those who suffer, and there lies its uniqueness and its challenge. Theology as "faith in search of understanding" seeks understanding from within suffering. While the analysis of poverty and its causes may be challenged, the choice of suffering as a point of departure for theology remains valid. Choosing suffering as a way into the Christian mystery ultimately leads to a fuller understanding not only of God as the mystery of justice and love, but of men and women who are to be prophets and mystics.

7
Ethics and Suffering: Stanley Hauerwas

Introduction

Dr. Stanley Hauerwas is professor of theological ethics at The Divinity School of Duke University. He is widely regarded as an important voice in the field of ethics. He has authored a host of articles and a number of books. One of his main preoccupations is the question of suffering and especially the suffering of children. Drawing on various stories of ill and dying individuals, especially children, he has attempted to clarify the basic theological and ethical issues connected with situations of suffering. In various ways Hauerwas has challenged the dominant paradigms of contemporary ethics and has provided many fresh insights relative to Christian ethics and the situation of suffering.

Suffering, for Hauerwas, is a basic and fundamental condition of human existence, and since morality is an essential aspect of human existence, "no account of the moral life which is worthy of our serious consideration can avoid asking us to endure suffering. Indeed the morally interesting question is not whether we are asked to suffer, but how and for what we are asked to suffer."[1] There is a moral significance to human suffering not simply because suffering cannot be avoided "but because the demands of morality cannot be satisfied without asking the self to submit to limits imposed by morality itself."[2] What Hauerwas is saying is that our inability to suffer would diminish our humanness.

Morality involves more than the capacity to think clearly and make rational decisions. "It is a way of seeing the world."[3] The world we see is a world marked by sufferings of all sorts. So ethics must be concerned with suffering. Hauerwas is in agreement with H. Richard Niebuhr that "suffering is a subject neglected by academic ethical theory and theological ethics, even though it is obviously present in each of our lives."[4]

The basic question that emerges in a situation of suffering has to do with the very nature of our personhood. As person we are truly subject to our suffering of our illness. As person we are constituted by our social interactions; we have a history, and what happens to us can be and should be integrated in our life story. As adults our sicknesses have a context and a life story. Without such a life-narrative, it then becomes very difficult to deal with suffering. As Hauerwas writes:

> I think childhood suffering bothers us so deeply because we assume that children lack a life story which potentially gives their illness some meaning. In that respect I suspect we often fail to appreciate the richness of their young world as well as their toughness and resilience. But I suspect that what bothers us even more about childhood suffering is that it makes us face our deepest suspicions that all of us lack a life story which would make us capable of responding to illness in a manner that would enable us to go on as individuals, as friends, as parents, and as a community. I suspect that if Christian convictions have any guidance to give us about how we are to understand as well as respond to suffering, it is by helping us discover that our lives are located in God's narrative—the God who has not abandoned us even when we or someone we care deeply about is ill.[5]

The Narrative Structure of Christianity

For Hauerwas, then, the way Christianity can respond to suffering is to offer a broad narrative: God's own narrative. This broad narrative is for the Christian centered on the person of Jesus.[6]

As Christians, our lives are made intelligible by participating and sharing in this particular history and particular narrative. Emphasis on narrative is theologically and ethically central for Christians. A narrative approach to Christian existence clearly manifests that such an existence is by essence contingent, that it depends on the previous existence of a community of faith, on a communal context. Theology and ethics never exist in the abstract; they never can be freed from narrative, nor from community. Christian ethics, then, is formed by a story with specific content. These narratives shape and sustain the faith community and the moral character of the participants. Moral identity for Hauerwas is fundamentally narrative in form, and narratives are of major significance for moral existence.[7] Yet not all narratives are equally valid and therefore some criteria must be established to judge and evaluate them. Hauerwas establishes the following criteria: "Any story we adopt or allow to adopt us will have to display (1) power to release us from destructive alternatives; (2) ways of seeing through current distortions; (3) room to keep us from having to resort to violence; and, finally, (4) a sense of the tragic: how meaning transcends power."[8] Christian ethics and theology are by nature traditional. They have to be "the imaginative endeavor to explicate the stories of God by showing how one claim illuminates another."[9]

The Function of Ethics

According to Hauerwas, "Theology is a practical activity concerned to display how Christian convictions construe the self and the world."[10] Ethics cannot be extraneous to the main task of theology; it is intrinsic to the believing community's theological task. "Christian ethics, insofar as it is an intelligible discipline at all, is dependent on a community's wisdom about how certain actions are prohibited or enjoined for the development of a particular kind of people."[11] This approach to ethics is clearly different from the more predominant ethics influenced by Kant: here being ethical implies being more fully rational.[12]

But Christian ethics like Aristotelian ethics are a matter of imitation.

> Christian ethics arise out of the formation of the peculiar
> community engendered by listening to scripture like the
> Sermon on the Mount and attaching ourselves to a master
> like Jesus.

In a sense within Christianity individuals are not simply called to be
moral "but faithful to the true story, the story that we are creatures
under the Lordship of a God who wants nothing more than our faithful
service."[14] From within this perspective, Christian ethics involves the
imaginative understanding of the Christian story. As Hauerwas writes:

> Christian ethics is the disciplined activity which analyzes
> and imaginatively tests the images most appropriate to
> orchestrate the Christian life in accordance with the central
> conviction that the world has been redeemed by the work
> of Jesus Christ. Christian ethics as such is not in principle
> methodologically different from other ethics, for I suspect
> all accounts of the moral life require some appeal to the
> virtues, principles, and the narrative display of each. What
> makes Christian ethics Christian is not our methodology,
> but the content of our convictions.[15]

From that perspective Christian ethics does not have as a goal to
confirm what every good person can know; it demands personal and
social transformation. Christian language like any other language can
only be understood on its own terms.

Christian ethics is determined by the very fact that Christian convictions "take the form of a story, or perhaps better, a set of stories that
constitute a tradition, which in turn creates and forms a community."[16]
For Hauerwas, the narrative mode is not accidental to Christian belief.
The most fundamental way of talking about God is through the story.

> The fact that we come to know God through the recounting
> of the story of Israel and the life of Jesus is decisive for our
> truthful understanding of the kind of God we worship as
> well as the world in which we exist. Put directly, the narra-
> tive character of our knowledge of God, the self, and the
> world is a reality-making claim that the world and our

> existence in it are God's creations; our lives and, indeed,
> the existence of the universe are but contingent realities.[17]

Even doctrines about God and Christ are themselves stories "because the Christian story is an enacted story. Liturgy is probably a much more important resource than are doctrines or creeds for helping us to hear and live the story of God."[18] Christian ethics cannot be free from its narrative and thus communal context. Emphasis on the narrative character of God's activity and the character of our existence reveals the nature of reality. We are, as Hauerwas writes, "destined to discover ourselves only within God's history, for God is our beginning and our end."[19] The enterprise of Christian ethics is to help us see. "We can only act within the world we can envision, and we can envision the world rightly only as we are trained to see. We do not come to see merely by looking, but must develop disciplined skills through initiation into that community that attempts to live faithful to the story of God...."[20]

Such an ethics based on the Christian narratives has no real interest in accommodating itself to various cultures. According to Hauerwas, one of the characteristics of American theology "has been its willingness, even avidity, to enter into dialogue with its culture."[21] Their basic quest is "to discern implicit or explicit 'religious significance' in the culture."[22] Now Hauerwas has not much sympathy for this kind of theology which he claims cannot be distinguished from journalism. Theology's concern with culture "has tended to trivialize the theological task."[23] What theology perceives as its task, the task of inculturation, Hauerwas sees in a negative way. "Thus theologians continue to foster the idea that the Church's mission is to translate the Gospel into the pieties of contemporary culture—that her mission is to spiritualize our civilization and our lives by identifying the current moralism with the meaningfulness of salvation."[24]

This is an improper understanding of the church's mission. "The Church is not called to build culture or to supply the moral tone of civilization, old or new. The Church is called to preach that the Kingdom of God has come close in the person and work of Jesus Christ."[25] The role of the church and of its theologians is that of the prophet: to stand apart and challenge. "Its task is to speak the word of truth amid warring spirits."[26] Relevancy has never been the formal criterion of truth.

"The Church does not exist to ask what needs doing to keep the world running smoothly and then to motivate our people to go do it."[27] The church has its own reason for being. The church should not be willing to suppress its peculiarities in order to participate responsibly in the culture.

Hauerwas' basic approach to ethics is the ongoing affirmation that Christianity is a particular way of relating to God, and that it is truly a useless task to translate its beliefs into terms that are meaningful and compelling for those who are not Christians. Such an approach is based on the false claim that a strong continuity exists between the God who redeems and the God who creates.

> By emphasizing the narrative character of our knowledge of God I mean to remind us that we do not know what it means to call God creator or redeemer apart from the story of his activity with Israel and Jesus. The language of creation and redemption, nature and grace, is a secondary theological language, that is sometimes mistaken for the story itself. "Creation" and "redemption" should be taken for what they are, namely ways of helping us tell and hear the story rightly.[28]

For Hauerwas, Jesus' cross calls into question any attempts to correlate the Christian message with any social and political order. All Christian ethics is necessarily transformative in nature; it indicates that the transformation of the self is necessary for any adequate account of the moral life. "For Christians the moral life, at least Scripturally, is seen as a journey through life sustained by fidelity to the cross of Christ, which brings a fulfillment no law can ever embody."[29] This implies that in Christianity, moral convictions have an "inherent historical and community-dependent nature."[30] Such moral convictions need to be carried from one generation to another through a community of believers. The beliefs that are intrinsically connected to ethics are "intelligible only if they are seen against the background of the Church—that is, a body of people who stand apart from the world because of the peculiar task of worshipping a God whom the world knows not."[31] While beliefs are important, what is of greater importance for Hauerwas is the kind of community these beliefs brought about. "To say they [the first Christians] believed in God is true but uninteresting. What is interesting is that they thought that their belief in God as they had encountered him in Jesus required the formation of a community distinct from the world exactly because of the kind of God he was. You cannot know what kind of God you disbelieve in, from a Christian perspective, unless you see what kind of community is necessary to worship him across time."[32] What is truly necessary is for the church to be a distinctive people. "As Christians we believe we not only need a community, but a community of a particular kind to live well morally."[33]

In ethics the first question is about seeing and not about doing. "The ethical task is not to tell you what is right or wrong but rather to train you to see. That explains why, in the Church, a great deal of time and energy are spent in the act of worship. In worship we are busy looking in the right direction."[34] The task of the church is to engender the right vision.

Ethics and Character

For Christian ethics, the character of the community is essential, and so is the character of the individual. By character he means "qualification of man's self-agency through his beliefs, intentions and actions, by which man acquires a moral history befitting his self-determining nature."[35] The formation of an ethical character is dependent on the sort of narrative available.

> Significant narratives produce significant and various characters necessary for the understanding and richness of the story itself. Just as scientific theories are partially judged by the fruitfulness of the activities they generate, so narratives can and should be judged by the richness of moral character and activity they generate. Or just as significant works of art occasion a tradition of interpretation and criticism, so significant narratives are at once the result of a continuation of moral communities and character that form nothing less than a tradition. And without tradition we have no means to ask questions of truth and falsity.[36]

The truth of the Christian narratives becomes a matter of the kind of life lived in relation to them.

> The emphasis on narrative as the grammar of religious convictions is an attempt to locate the question of the truthfulness of religious convictions without losing the insistence that the moral force of those claims is essential for their truthfulness.[37]

The ethics of character is an attempt "to shift the focus on decision, to the relation between belief and behavior, thought and action."[38] So the fundamental issue in ethics "is not just what we do but what we are and how what we are is formed by our fundamental convictions about the nature and significance of Christ."[39] So Christian ethics is by necessity intrinsically connected to every other aspect of theology, "since how the nature of Christ and his work is understood and the various Christian symbols are related make a difference for the orientation of the Christian's character."[40]

Behind Hauerwas' emphasis on character lies an agency theory of the self. The self is more active than passive. "We are who we are because our actions are formed by how our attention is directed through our language and symbols."[41] "Our character is thus the qualification of our self-agency through our beliefs, intentions and actions through which we acquire an ongoing orientation."[42] Since we are by essence social beings, we can acquire our characters. "The kind of character we have is therefore relative to the kind of community from which we inherit our primary symbols and practices."[43]

The character of the Christian is formed and nurtured in the Christian community. In fact, "The nature of community also determines the nature and function of ethical discourse and argument."[44] One of the community's tasks is to provide individuals with the proper reasons for specific ethical actions. Now those reasons are not only appropriate for determining what is right or wrong ethically, but they imply a whole way of life. Here the community's central symbols play a significant role in establishing a meaningful dimension of life. These symbols central to the community's existence provide the individual with unity and cohesion over long periods of time. For Hauerwas, "The Christian life is not solely a matter of doing but of seeing and hearing.... The task of Christian ethics is to help keep the grammar of the language of faith pure so we may claim not only to speak the truth but also to embody that truth in our lives."[45]

Ethics and Suffering

Now for Stanley Hauerwas, there is a basic relationship between Christian ethics, as he understands it, and human suffering. In his book, *Naming the Silences*, Stanley Hauerwas elaborates basic relations between ethics and suffering. In the preface of the book, the author states his intention on focusing "primarily on why the problem of illness and death—particularly the problem of childhood illness and death—is so troubling for us."[46] While clearly such a focusing must somehow touch on the theodicy question, the author makes no attempt to explain such evil or to explain why a good and all-powerful God allows us to undergo suffering for seemingly no reason. In fact any attempt to justify God "is a theological mistake."[47] The author is interested in the connection between suffering and the sufferer's relation to God: Why is it when one is faced with basic situations of suffering there is a need for an explanation? "It is almost as if we have a primitive need to know that such an illness or death does not render our existence and God's existence absurd."[48] For Hauerwas, such a "primitive" need is "based on destructive presuppositions about the nature of our existence."[49]

The book is intended to help people name the powers that they think they have under control. The book is an attempt "to show how the God whom Christians worship can give a voice to their pain."[50] Basically the goal intended is not to give an explanation of evil "when what is required is a community capable of absorbing our grief."[51] Relative to suffering, Hauerwas claims and confirms H.R. Niebuhr's statement:

> Because suffering is the exhibition of the presence in our existence of that which is not under our control, or of the intrusion into our self-legislating existence of an activity operating under another law than ours, it cannot be brought adequately within spheres of teleological or deontological ethics. Yet it is in response to suffering that many and per-

haps all men . . . define themselves, take on character, develop their ethos.[52]

The Nature of Suffering

There is a common assumption that since suffering is such a universal phenomenon, it does not need to be analyzed in depth. For Hauerwas, suffering is "an extremely elusive subject."[53] Suffering most forcefully connotes for Hauerwas a passive element. To suffer means to undergo, to be subjected to the negative. "Suffering has as its root sense the idea of submitting or being forced to submit to endure some particular set of circumstances. Thus we usually think of the sufferer as being a victim or patient."[54] Again Hauerwas writes, "We suffer when what we undergo blocks our positive desires and wants."[55] Suffering also connotes a reality in our lives that simply cannot be recycled; nothing good or other can emerge from suffering. "Suffering also carries a sense of 'surdness': it denotes those frustrations for which we can give no satisfying explanation and which we cannot make serve some wider end. Suffering thus names a sense of brute power that does violence to our best laid plans. It is not easily domesticated."[56] So suffering cannot simply be described; there is always a question about purpose and value. Suffering also has a more active sense—like that of "bearing with, permitting, or enduring."[57] So suffering cannot simply be associated with a reality over which we have no power and for which we can do nothing.

This passive and active aspect of suffering leads us to understand that there are different kinds of suffering. For Hauerwas, "We must distinguish between those forms of suffering that happen to us and those that we bring on ourselves or that are requisite to our purpose and goals."[58] Pain and illness are a form of suffering that "seem to stand on that side of suffering that is more a matter of fate than choice."[59] They reduce the sufferer to the level of victim. So there are realities from which we suffer and over which we have no control. But there are also realities which cause us suffering and over which we do have some control. "This latter sense of 'suffer,' moreover, seems more subjective, since what may appear as a problem for one may seem an opportunity for another. Not only is what we suffer relative to our projects, but how we suffer is relative to what we have or wish to be."[60] Yet the distinctions between these two forms of suffering should not be pressed too much. "Our increasing knowledge of the relation of illness to life-style is enough to make us think twice before drawing a hard and fast distinction between what happens to us and what we do."[61]

Pain and suffering often alienate us from others, and from ourselves. They turn us into strangers, into people we do not recognize. Part of the process of dealing with suffering is for the sufferer to name the suffering. "The very ability to name what they have seems to give them a sense of control or possession that replaces the undifferentiated fear they had been feeling."[62] Suffering has an alienating effect. "By its very nature suffering alienates us not only from one another but from ourselves, especially suffering which we undergo, which is not easily integrated into our ongoing projects or hopes. To suffer is to have our identity threatened physically, psychologically, and morally. Thus our suffering even makes us unsure of who we are."[63]

For Hauerwas it is not a question of always having to transform suffering into benefit. "We rightly feel that some forms of suffering can only be acknowledged not transformed."[64] Some forms of suffering are so extreme that they can only be acknowledged. "Certain kinds of suffering—Hiroshima, Auschwitz, wars—are so horrible we are able to preserve our humanity only by denying them human significance. No 'meaning' can be derived from the Holocaust except that we must do everything we can to see that it does not happen again."[65] Other forms can be acknowledged and transformed. For Hauerwas, though, the most important question has to do basically with the sufferer, with the character of the sufferer. "More important is the question of what kind of people we ought to be so that certain forms of suffering are not denied but accepted as part and parcel of our existence as moral agents."[66] Again relative to suffering, "The issue is not what we do, but rather who we ought to be in order to be capable of accepting all suffering as a necessary aspect of human existence. In viewing our life narrowly as a matter of purposes and accomplishments, we may miss our actual need for suffering, even apparently purposeless or counter-purposeful suffering."[67]

Suffering and Acceptance

For Hauerwas the refusal to accept certain suffering or the attempt to interpret and give human meaning to other forms of suffering "is essential for our moral health."[68] It seems that suffering is the destiny of all human reality. But the question does pose itself as to the "why" of our suffering. For Hauerwas, "We suffer because we are incomplete beings who depend on one another for our existence." So it is our interdependence that causes our suffering. "Suffering is built into our condition because it is literally true that we exist only to the extent that we sustain, or 'suffer,' the existence of others and the others include not just others like us, but mountains, trees, animals, and so on."[69] What makes suffering so difficult is that it goes against some of our cherished assumptions about our own identity, especially about our independence. Yet there is an irony built into our ability to suffer, and that is that our neediness is also the basic source of our strength. "For our need requires the cooperation and love of others from which derives our ability not only to live but to flourish."[70]

One basic question consistently posed by Hauerwas in different contexts concerns the necessity to alleviate or remove suffering. This question is usually asked in connection with the medical profession's adherence to the principle of alleviating suffering as an unqualified obligation. Hauerwas' questions are: "Why should we assume that existence is only valuable when it is free of suffering? Why should we assume that we should always try to spare the other suffering when we know that often the good we do comes only because we were willing to endure pain?"[71] Hauerwas is not advocating that suffering should be sought out. His is not a masochistic position; suffering is not an inherent good. "Rather I am trying to suggest that though suffering is not to be sought, neither must we assume it should always be avoided. Often we achieve the good only because we are willing to endure in ourselves and others an existence of suffering and pain."[72]

The Question of Theodicy

Not every form of suffering is an evil; some suffering necessarily follows the making of our own ethical character. Yet there is a suffering that cannot be easily made sense of, such as the suffering of the

innocent, or the suffering of children. Such suffering does pose the
fundamental theodicy question. Hauerwas affirms that he is skeptical
of most theodicies. Most theodicies are false since they are related to a
false understanding of God's power. Such a belief leads to the presumption that nothing bad should really happen to such believers: there
is a "deep-seated presumption that our belief in God is irrational if it
does not put us on the winning side of history."[73] His basic thesis is that
while suffering is real yet there is no such thing as suffering that challenges belief in the existence of God as such. "The problem of evil is
not about rectifying our suffering with some general notion of God's
nature as all-powerful and good; rather, it is about what we mean by
God's goodness itself, which for Christians must be construed in terms
of God as the Creator who has called into existence a people called
Israel so that the world might know that God has not abandoned us.
There is no problem of suffering in general; rather, the question of suffering can be raised only in the context of a God who creates to
redeem."[74] Only within a specific context, a specific narrative, a community of belief, can there be a valid approach to the fundamental
questions posed by the suffering of the innocent. Our existence finds
meaning only within the Christian narrative.[75] This narrative involves a
concept of God that offers no real solution to the question of suffering.[76]

For Hauerwas, suffering always occurs within an interpretative
context, for suffering is always occasioned by something, and our ability to recognize our suffering means that suffering always takes place
in an interpretative context. There is no abstract suffering and no
abstract answer. We always suffer from some particular reality and in a
particular context. In order to recognize suffering an interpretative context is necessary.[77]

The Meaning of the Cross

Christianity's response to suffering, or, better still Christianity as
an interpretative framework, must be the "ongoing narrative of God's
redemption of creation through the cross and resurrection of Christ."[78]
It is within this interpretative framework, this ongoing narrative, that
our affirmation of God's suffering must be placed. Such an understanding of God as a suffering God can help us deal with the develop-

mentally disabled. According to Hauerwas, "God's face is the face of the retarded; God's body is the body of the retarded; God's being is that of the retarded."[79] Hauerwas' God is not the all-powerful, immutable and absolutely independent God. God is characterized by self-giving love, by freely accepted interdependence. "Unlike us, God is not separated from himself or us by his suffering; rather, his suffering makes it possible for him to share our life and for us to share his."[80] Again in a more explicit way Hauerwas affirms that "the God we Christians worship is the God of the sacrifice, the God of weakness and suffering, who draws us to his table not by coercive but by sacrificial love."[81] The freely accepted weakness of God is made manifest in the death on the cross. God provides for us in the crucified Jesus "a Saviour who teaches us how to be weak without regret."[82] In the paschal mystery we are offered a narrative "that helps us sustain the task of charity in a world where it can never be successful."[83]

The cross challenges any attempt at making effectiveness the goal of the Christian life. It is not that the cross is simply a sign of the Christian's quiet, suffering submission to the existing powers; for the "Cross stands as God's (and our) eternal "no" to the powers of death, as well as God's eternal "yes" to humanity, God's remarkable determination not to leave us to our own devices."[84] So the suffering of Christ becomes for the Christian the way to deal with their own suffering. Quoting Romans, Hauerwas writes concerning Paul's invitation to "rejoice in our suffering":

> This seems to indicate that for the early Christians suffering was but an opportunity for living in a way more faithful to the new age which they believed had begun in Christ. Their suffering did not make them question their belief in God, much less God's goodness; their suffering only confirmed their belief that they were part of Christ's church through baptism into his death. Their faith gave them a way to go on in the face of specific persecution and general misfortune. Suffering, even their suffering from evil and injustice, did not create a metaphysical problem needing solution; rather, it was a practical challenge requiring a communal response.[85]

Yet Paul's invitation should not be understood as making suffering an end in itself or lead us to the too easy acceptance of suffering that can be alleviated. Distinctions must be made in the various forms of our suffering. It is important to distinguish the forms of suffering that emerge from faithfulness to the cross and those that do not. "The suffering that is a consequence of our living a faithful life has a different valence than that which is not."[86] The difference in the suffering lies in the fact that they are the consequences of choosing a way of life. This kind of suffering is named from the beginning because we have a sense of the way it is happening. And while the cross provides the Christian a pattern of interpretation, the meaningfulness of the Christ story for suffering cannot be imposed on others who do not share the same narrative. It is also possible that this story gives us "too much understanding." Christians "are under no obligation to interpret all their misfortunes by identifying them with Christ's Cross."[87] Such an application of the cross can lead to self-deception and to the trivialization of the cross by using it as a universal symbol for the "surdness" of suffering.[88] While one should not be seeking the cross, it is possible for someone to accept suffering as part of one's ministry to the world.[89]

Suffering, especially that caused by illness, does challenge our sense of autonomy, our basic presumption that we are in charge of our existence and directors of our destiny. It seems of real importance for us to be able to name the causes of our suffering, for this gives us the impression of control. Every sickness also evokes death over which we have no power. Yet because suffering is a threat to our autonomy, it is an important factor in the making of our moral self.[90]

An essential rule of the Judeo-Christian narrative is to help us name the silences that our suffering has created and to give us the capacity to accept our "inexplicable suffering and pain."[91]

Conclusion

To be ethical in a Christian way is to be dependent on the church; loyalty to one's ecclesial community. Christian ethics is dependent on specific narratives and, therefore, is by essence specific and distinct from other ethics. Emphasis on the distinctiveness of Christian ethics does not lead to claims of superiority or to the denial of points of contact with other forms of ethics. But for Hauerwas, there can be no universal ground for Christian ethics, no natural law standpoint independent of the narrative. Moral existence is dependent on narrative, for all agency has a basic historical character. My moral and ethical "I" is formed and dependent on a specific community formed by specific narratives; for Stanley Hauerwas, the Christian's first loyalty and moral obligation is to his or her community. To become an ethical person is to learn a language, to accept a vision. The ethical person is on a "journey of intensification." In this journey there can be no freedom from the narrative, nor from the communal context; the journey demands a process of socialization into highly particular outlooks. This approach has important implications for any theological-ethical approach to suffering. Basically only the converted person can fully deal with suffering. Stanley Hauerwas is in agreement with the following statement from Kenneth Surin:

> The "unconverted person's endeavors to resolve the 'problem of evil,' no matter how sincere and intellectually gifted this person might be, are doomed ultimately to be self-defeating. Only faith in Christ makes possible the cleansing of our vision, a cleansing regarded by Augustine as the necessary preliminary to the vision of God." Without such conversion, "the very process of seeking to answer the question 'whence is evil?' will be undermined by the distorted thinking of a crippled intellect."[92]

There are no abstract or universal perspectives to suffering; the answer to suffering lies not in a set of beliefs but in a set of convictions about God's graciousness revealed in the redeeming death of Jesus, requiring conversion and belonging to a faithful community. Such an approach has been described as "withdrawal" ethics, or even "withdrawal" theology. Such withdrawals involve a stance of standing apart from society and that of witnessing to the society at large. There is little common ground between the "church's" position and that of society and of other religious traditions. Dialogue is not of prime importance; yet, since suffering is such a universal reality and since the causes of much suffering lie in social structures, a stance of "withdrawal" does not appear to be justifiable.

If the Christian narratives do address the question of suffering in a vital and meaningful way, they cannot be perceived to be important "only" for those who are converted. Meaningfulness as it relates to suffering cannot simply be sectarian in nature. There are too many elements—biological, social, psychological—that go into the making of meaning in a situation of suffering so that a restrictive approach cannot be sufficient.

Meaning for suffering can receive plausibility from sources other than those of the Christian community. The truth claims of the Christian narratives, relative to their understanding of suffering, cannot be purely subjective and valid only for those socialized into Christian culture and language. Here I must agree with James Gustafson when he writes:

> It is God with whom humankind has to reckon; God who is the source of all life, whose powers have brought it into being, sustain it, bear down upon it, create conditions of possibility within it and will determine its ultimate destiny. Theology has to be open to all the sources that help us to construe God's relations to the world; ethics has to deal with the interdependence of all things in relation to God. This, for me, necessarily relativizes the significance of the Christian tradition, though it is the tradition in which our theologies develop. God is the God of Christians, but God is not a Christian God for Christians only.[93]

Conclusion

Introduction

What has emerged in the previous chapters is that according to many contemporary theologians, the task of theology is to a large extent dictated by the universal experience of suffering. While theology can be defined in various ways, any fruitful theology must at least be a reflection on how the basic Christian's symbols, especially that of the paschal mystery, affect our self-understanding in our relation to the world and to God. Human existence can be grasped from various perspectives. Our theologians perceive human existence primarily in its encounter with the experience of negativity; what gives rise to theological reflection is the experience of suffering. Theology is always about humanity and God; and the most important question about God is whether God makes a difference in the world, in our lives. The greatest obstacle in answering this question is the existence of the suffering of the innocent, which can only be perceived as an evil. The greatest argument against the existence of an omnipotent and all-loving God is the existence of evil; there can be no escape from theodicy. No word about God is ultimately valid that cannot be offered in the presence of suffering children.

Theology in a Context

The one constant characterizing the theologians we have surveyed is that their theology is contextual. A contextual theology is one that emphasizes the place-dimension of the human condition. "Place" here is not to be understood only as a geographical reality; it also refers in a more metaphysical way to personal presence: to be a woman in a male-dominated culture; to be poor and homeless in an affluent society; to be old in a youth-centered culture. Suffering is such a place, such a space; it is a basic context which challenges theology. Contextualization involves a methodological shift. There is no way one can take suffering seriously without changing one's theological approach.

Coping with the negativities of life appears to be the acid test not only of the Christian faith but also of its theology. This has been sharply expressed by Ernest Becker: "Whatever man does on this planet has to be done in the lived truth of the terror of the rumble of panic underneath everything. Otherwise it is false."[1] Not to consider suffering is to mutilate theology in its very essence. Suffering has a priority in theology; for what is truly at stake is not simply our humanness but also our Christian faith.[2]

The Theodicy Question

A theology which originates in suffering makes itself very vulnerable—the vulnerability arising from the theodicy question.[3] There is an intractability about suffering; there can be no easy answers. One thing the authors we have surveyed have in common is that they all take human suffering very seriously and refuse to offer easy answers. In every theological explanation of suffering, the scandal of the suffering of the innocent remains. The existence of suffering is an ongoing obstacle to any form of utopianism; it opposes reductionism at all levels. For Gutierrez and Schillebeeckx, suffering eliminates the possibility of reducing all thought either to the practical or to the contemplative. Suffering demands resistance and opposition; but since it is ultimately intractable, suffering demands a basic contemplative stance and language.

Theology and Experience

The difficulty that suffering poses for theology is also most evident when experience is seen as an essential point of departure for all theological inquiry. The basic source of conflict between experience and theology is that experience is ambiguous, personal, affective, whereas theology aims to be a rational and coherent discourse about God and reality. Experiences are narrated; theology exposes. Such conflict is most evident when the experience is about suffering. There is no acceptable order to the ways that suffering impinges upon human experience. There is no telling when we are to be brought low by suffering, reduced to impotence in our quest for fulfillment. We live consistently under the threat of chaos; we often have difficulty in making sense of this world. It is not hard to understand why the one who is suffering and cannot make sense of his world will be suspicious of any theological system that pretends to put order in a disordered world. Those who suffer have much difficulty in making sense of the world. Their response to the given reality is complex, often made of faith, acceptance, and a large dose of pretense. Theologians cannot simply pretend to have ultimate answers to the why of suffering. The truth here is that there is a built-in resistance to theology in the reality of suffering and that built-in resistance has to do with the intractability of the theodicy question. There are no purely abstract approaches to the question of suffering and therefore also to theodicy. Such abstraction about suffering can truly reduce the full human dimension of suffering and lead to apathy. When it comes to the question of suffering, faith and reason do not lie down quietly together. Theology must be a critical and painful examination of God's word about suffering and man's/woman's words about suffering.

Suffering: Cause and Meaning

While there is much agreement on how suffering affects theology, theologians do differ on two fundamental issues: the cause or causes of suffering and the meaningfulness of suffering. These two issues are interconnected. One's position on the origin of suffering will clearly affect the question of meaningfulness. Suffering has its origin, according to our authors, in the human condition, in personal sinfulness, in structures of sinfulness; so suffering can be perceived in a very personal way or in a more collective way such as the suffering of a group of people. Suffering can also be understood as an element of the historical process or in more ontological form such as an intrinsic and essential dimension of human existence. The meaningfulness or mean-inglessness of suffering according to most of the theologians we have surveyed depends on whether suffering can or cannot be alleviated or even eliminated. Yet the question of meaning lingers on: Is there a value in suffering? Can theology uncover such meaning? Can we sim-ply accept Gutierrez's affirmation that the main purpose of Job's suf-fering was to correct his "myopic view of God."[4] The basic answer given by Christianity is that suffering can be redemptive; our redemp-tion has been accomplished in and through the suffering of Jesus Christ. The suffering of the innocent can be offered up for others. In Pope John Paul II's letter on "The Christian Meaning of Human Suffering" of February 1989, one finds a summary of the Catholic tra-dition on the nature of suffering. Writing about Jesus' suffering, the pope affirms: "It seems to be part of the very essence of Christ's redemptive suffering that this suffering requires to be unceasingly completed." The Pope continues: "Suffering is something good before which the Church bows down in reverence with all the depth of her faith in the redemption."[5]

Suffering: A Feminist Approach

This interpretation is radically opposed by feminist theologians.[6] For Soelle, Christianity's approach to suffering is often masochistic. Is it necessary, she asks, that the image of Christ on the cross communi-cate the message that suffering is redemptive, and therefore attractive? In fact, for many feminist theologians, Christianity's understanding of redemption is the primary reason so many women are acculturated to accept abuse. According to Mary Daly, "The qualities that Christianity idealizes, especially for women, are also those of a victim: sacrificial love, passive acceptance of suffering, humility, meekness, etc. Since these are the qualities idealized in Jesus 'who died for our sins,' his functioning as a model reinforces the scapegoat syndrome for women."[7]

Is there any other way of grasping the meaning of the cross? Clearly such authors as Soelle, Schillebeeckx, and Gutierrez view the mystery of the cross as one of redemptive love. For Schillebeeckx, Jesus was a victim on the cross; he suffered the consequences of his commitment to compassionate love. "No one has greater love than this to lay down one's life for one's friends" (Jn 15:6).

The Pain of God

In order to avoid a masochistic understanding of God, some of our authors have affirmed that suffering is not only humanity's destiny but also the destiny of God. It has been suggested that the notion of a "suffering God" is becoming a new orthodoxy in the twentieth century. While the ongoing affirmation of the tradition has been the immutability and impassibility of God, many contemporary theologians are now emphasizing a different understanding of God much in line with A. Whitehead's God as fellow-sufferer. God is so intimately involved with creation, God's love is such that it becomes theologically incoherent to keep referring to the impassibility of God. A truly "living God" cannot be reconciled to affirmations of impassibility. In the story of the disciples of Emmaus, the risen Lord is one who accompanies the suffering disciples. The emphasis on a suffering God does change Christianity's approach to suffering and its notion of atonement. It does highlight the fundamental biblical affirmation that God is compassionate. "Be as compassionate as I am compassionate."

For western thought, whose roots lie in Athens, reality is substantialistic; for the biblical tradition reality is through and through relational. The biblical ontology is not about being as such, but about *being-with*, and therefore it also presupposes the genuine prospect of not being-with, of being-against, and being-alone, in short, of discontinuity. Such a relational ontology has been advocated by process theology. The fundamental response of process theology to the situation of human suffering has been the affirmation of a bipolar God, a God who in one of God's poles can suffer. If God is a loving God as scripture affirms, then God must suffer.[8] The process-God is not one of stony impassibility; God is a living God, the "fellow sufferer who understands" and is bound in an intimate way with creation, in its moaning and suffering. Far from causing suffering, God endures self-suffering.

This understanding of God as one who suffers can have many meanings; not all of them are fully acceptable. We have already seen how Moltmann's position on the death of Jesus has been resisted by Soelle and Schillebeeckx.

The suffering-God approach leads us to change our understanding of God's power, and therefore to qualify our understanding of God's omnipotence. Such a change clearly affects the theodicy enigma which has been expressed classically in three propositions: (1) God is all-powerful, (2) God is all-good, and (3) the innocent do suffer. The suffering-God approach also provides us with one more resource in our theology of suffering, and this one can be characterized as pastoral, a practical one. It has to do with the practice of compassionate care for the afflicted. What is being affirmed here is the role of human solidarity in the transformation of suffering. Compassionate care for the suffering addresses the basic cause of most suffering.

The Paschal Mystery and the Power of God

The affirmation that God does truly suffer poses a basic question about the nature of God's power and also human power. If we say that God suffers with us, is this the last word about God? If suffering is projected in God's eternity, what hope remains of eliminating suffering in this world? Is our God impotent? If not, what is the nature of God's power? Soelle has already made the point that only the suffering that can be changed can have meaning. According to Daniel Day Williams, "Suffering in the being of God is not just any suffering; it is the supreme instance of the transmutation of suffering."[9] God being God only suffers as God, not as a creature. Yet, that God truly suffers poses the question about God's power, about power itself. Within the perspective of a suffering God, God's power must be of an other order than that of domination or coercion. God's power as manifest in the paschal mystery works through suffering and love and forgiveness, and when measured on the scale of political power can seem to be weakness.

What the paschal mystery leads to is a different understanding of power. Power is usually associated with domination, competition and control. Max Weber's classic definition reads: "Power is the probability that one actor in a social relationship will be in a position to carry out his own will despite resistance, regardless of the basis on which this probability rests."[10] Here the increase in power of the one entails a decrease in power—and therefore, in freedom, equality and solidarity—of the other. In ordinary social science, power "is the ability to influence, guide, adjust, manipulate, shape, control or transform the human or natural environment in order to advance one's purposes—whether the actual exercise of power is direct or indirect, coercive or persuasive."[11] Power is seen as a linear, one-way process. A linear definition of power is anthropologically problematic. It perceives the self as having an individuality and substantive nature. Such a power is never voluntarily given up. As John Coleman writes, "linear views of power sustain and nurture selfishness, the unregulated conflict of interest, will with will."[12] Such a definition leads to a voluntaristic decisionist understanding of the world. A dominant group can more or less spontaneously surrender power and prerogative but only if these have become superfluous, troublesome or dangerous. In this definition of power, the powerful define the powerless and in this defining the powerless lose independence and authentic identity.

The paschal mystery does not see power as domination or as coercion. In 1 Corinthians 1:18-25, Paul presents the crucified Christ as the power of God and as the wisdom of God. God chooses powerlessness and weakness and therefore challenges the prevailing canons of wisdom: "Has not God made foolish the wisdom of the age" (1:20). For, according to Paul, "the foolishness of God is wiser than men and the weakness of God is stronger than men" (1:25). In Philippians 2, the self-emptying of Jesus is the revelation that to be God is to be unselfishness itself. In his life, Jesus pursued a style of service even to the act of total self-giving. He did so not simply as a model of conduct but as revealer of divine reality. Being God means being giver and gift, the ever-creative author of all goodness. God can know no holding back, no selfishness, no fear or loss of power. For God, no dichotomy exists between creative power and saving grace. As revealer of that power Jesus came "not to be served but to serve" (Mk 10:45). To experience God's salvific power is to reject other forms of salvation as capable of transforming humans and bringing them to their destiny. As 1 John 3:14 proclaims, the presence of this power as unselfish love (agape) transforms death to life and places believers in conflict with every human attempt to manipulate reality.

In the theology of the cross Mark demonstrates that in the final analysis God's power is the power to renounce power. In other words it is only through God's power that Jesus is able to allow himself to become powerless and face the necessity of the cross. The renouncing of power is for the empowerment of Jesus in the resurrection. God's power cannot properly be understood except in terms of its opposite, powerlessness. God's power is to renounce power. According to Mark it is through God's power that Jesus is able to become powerless and submit to death. Dorothy Lee-Pollard writes: "The divine power by which Jesus in the Gospels heals and liberates others is the same power by which he is able to renounce the power to save his own life."[13] Again, according to the same author:

> So that breath-taking power to renounce power—to renounce what is most precious, what alone gives purpose and meaning to life, what lies at the core of one's identi- ty—is precisely what reveals and actualizes the power of God. That is why the centurion recognizes who Jesus is in the blackness and despair of his death.[14]

What is true of Jesus is also true of discipleship. It is God's power that enables them to relinquish power. God can empower even the rich to give up their wealth for the sake of the poor.

Power according to the paschal mystery is not something to be held onto; it is essentially relational and self-sacrificial. In Rollo May's terms, it is integrative power. It envisions mutuality and reciprocity— neither power over, nor power against, nor power for, but power with.[15] The power proposed in the paschal mystery is advocated by Bernard Loomer:

> The capacity to absorb an influence is as truly a mark of power as the strength involved in exercising an influence. Power is the capacity to sustain a relationship. This is the relationship of influencing and being influenced, of giving and receiving, of making claims and permitting and enabling others to make their claims.[16]

Loomer's model of power is one that is relational where selves and groups emerge as realities. The magnitude of power consists in "the range and depth of relationships that we can sustain."[17] This includes relationships of receptivity and even suffering, not the positing of one will against another will. Power is relation, and therefore the more power, the more not the less relations. So in a real sense there is never power without responsibility.[18] As power and freedom are correlative notions, so are power and responsibility.

The personal world is a world of mutual reciprocity and equality between agents. Thus there exists a mutual enhancement of personal powers when the personal world and its agents are operating cointentionally, that is, cooperatively. When a condition of cooperation is vitiated or absent, a situation of domination usually ensues. A condition of domination is operating when the agency of one person or group eclipses or masks the agency of another person or group; such domination is oppression. In a situation of oppression the agency of one person or group denies the possibility of the other person's or group's consciousness, intentionality, intentions, responsibility and significance. A relationship of domination creates powerlessness in the dominated person or group. Evil is the consequence of disparities of power because where disparity of power is great, violence or control by coercion is the predominant mode of social interaction. Evil is the active or passive effort to deny or suppress another's power-of-being-in-relation. A society where power inequity prevails perpetuates deep woundedness in the lives of its members. Those who are "outsiders" to the predominant power base and values of that society are seen to be and therefore experience themselves as worthless.

Conclusion

Christianity's approach to suffering and negativity is to offer a narrative, a complex of symbols, the paschal mystery, which can permit a realistic viewing of the world, without succumbing to meaninglessness. The theological journey of our authors begins with the experience of suffering which, while secular in nature, somehow calls for a religious symbolization. The theology of our authors is to think through and elaborate a perspective of suffering which is illuminated by and oriented in terms of the resources made available in the paschal mystery. The real test of the viability of the vision of the paschal mystery is its capacity to provide insight and guidance in an overwhelming situation of suffering. The interpretation of the theologians we have considered, which is not perfect or complete, can nurture contemporary individuals and society as they attempt to cope with various experiences of suffering. Their task as theologians has been to safeguard belief and hope in the compassionate and redeeming love of God. It is the task of making possible for all generations Paul's own faith/hope experience: "For I am convinced that neither death, nor life, nor angels, nor rulers, nor things present, nor things to come, nor powers, nor height, nor depth, nor anything else in all creation will be able to separate us from the love of God in Christ Jesus our Lord" (Rom 8:38-39).

Notes

Introduction

1. Viktor Frankl, *Man's Search for Meaning: An Introduction to Logotherapy* (Boston: Beacon Press, 1959).

2. Clifford Geertz, *The Interpretation of Cultures* (New York: Basic Books, 1973) p. 312.

3. Ibid. p. 90.

4. George A. Lindbeck, *The Nature of Doctrine* (Philadelphia: The Westminster Press, 1984) p. 32.

5. Paul Tillich, *Systematic Theology* (Chicago: University of Chicago Press, 1963) III:227.

6. Clifford Geertz, *The Interpretation of Cultures*, op. cit. p. 103.

7. Ibid. p. 104.

8. John Paul II, "The Christian Meaning of Human Suffering" in *Origins* Feb. 23, 1984, vol. 13, no. 37, p. 620

9. Martin Luther King, Jr., quoted in *A Testament of Hope,* ed. James Washington (New York: Harper & Row, 1986), p. 47.

10. Edward Schillebeeckx, *Jesus: An Experiment in Christology* (New York: Crossroad, 1979) p. 621.

11. Stanley Hauerwas, *Naming the Silences: God, Medicine and the Problem of Suffering* (Grand Rapids: William B. Eerdmans Publishing Co., 1990) p. 148.

12. C.S. Lewis, *A Grief Observed* (London: Bantam Books, 1976) p. 5.

13. Harold Kushner, *When Bad Things Happen to Good People* (New York: Avon Books, 1983) p. 4.

14. As J. Moltmann writes: "The suffering of a single innocent child is an irrefutable rebuttal of the notion of the almighty and kindly God in heaven. For a God who lets the innocent suffer and who permits senseless death is not worthy to be called a God at all. Wherever the suffering of the living in all its manifold forms pierces our consciousness with pain, we lose our childish primal confidence and our trust in God." In Jürgen Moltmann, *Trinity and Kingdom* (New York: Harper Row, 1981) p. 47.

15. As Langdon Gilkey writes: "Systematic theology is the mutual interpretation of experienced questions and symbolic answers, the one being a means for the understanding of the other.... Meaning is an interpretation of symbol and *experience*, and so in religious meaning an interaction of the experience of the sacred with religious symbols which *mediate* and *thematize* the experience." In "New Modes of Empirical Theology" in *The Future of Empirical Theology*, ed. Bernard E. Meland (Chicago: University of Chicago Press, 1969) p. 367.

16. Walter Kasper, *The God of Jesus Christ* (New York: Crossroad, 1984) p. 84.

17. Gustavo Gutierrez, *On Job: God-Talk and the Suffering of the Innocent* (Maryknoll: Orbis Press, 1987) p. 102.

18. Dorothy Soelle, *The Strength of the Weak. Toward a Christian Feminist Identity* (Philadelphia: The Westminster Press, 1984) p. 90.

19. Carter Heyward in *Christianity in Crisis,* Dec. 11 (1989) p. 381.

20. Walter Kasper, *The God of Jesus Christ,* op. cit. p. 160.

21. Ibid.

22. Arthur C. McGill, *Suffering: A Test of Theological Method* (Philadelphia: Geneva Press, 1968) p. 158.

23. Raymond Panikkar, *The Intra-Religious Dialogue* (New York: Paulist, 1978) p. 78.

24. Here one must agree with Paul Tillich's claim that all theology is existential: "All theological statements are existential. They imply the man who makes the statement or who asks the question. The creaturely existence of which theology speaks is 'my' creaturely

existence, and only on this basis is the consideration of creatureliness in general meaningful. This existential correlation is abandoned if the question of theodicy is raised with respect to persons other than the questioner." In Paul Tillich, *Systematic Theology* (Chicago: University of Chicago, 1966) 1:269.

25. Sallie McFague, *Models of God. Theology for an Ecological, Nuclear Age* (Philadelphia: Fortress Press, 1987) pp.ix-x.

26. Paul van Buren writes: "Auschwitz raises questions about the victory of the cross over death. In the fact of that Kingdom of Death, can it now be said that death is swallowed up in victory? In the light of this unparalleled manifestation of corruption, can it now be said that the corruption of creation has been remedied? Can the Suffering Servant of Isaiah 53 be taken any longer to refer to solely to the suffering Jew on the Cross, when we have seen photographs of the deadened faces and stacked, corpses of God's people in the death camps? Auschwitz surely makes these questions morally and theologically unavoidable for the Church, however difficult it may be to answer them. *A Theology of the Jewish-Christian Reality* (San Francisco: Harper & Row, 1988) p. 139.

27. David Tracy in the Foreward of Arthur Cohen's *The Tremendum: A Theological Interpretation of the Holocaust* (New York: Crossroad, 1981) p. vii.

28. Robert Lifton and Eric Olson, *Living and Dying* (New York: Praeger, 1974) p. 137.

29. Christopher Lash, *The Culture of Narcissism* (London: Abacus, 1980) pp. 36–41.

1. A Biblical View of Suffering: Walter Brueggemann

1. Colin Gunton. "Using and Being Used: Scripture and Systematic Theology" in *Theology Today*, vol. XLVII, no. 3, Oct. (1990) p. 251.

2. Ibid. p. 257

3. Walter Brueggemann, *Israel's Praise. Doxology Against Idolatry and Ideology* (Philadelphia: Fortress Press, 1988) p. 129.

4. Walter Brueggemann, "The Rhetoric of Hurt and Hope: Ethics Odd and Crucial" in *The Annual of the Society of Christian Ethics*, pp. 88–89.

5. Ibid.

6. Ibid. p. 72.

7. Walter Brueggemann, *Revelation and Violence: A Study in Contextualization* (Milwaukee: Marquette University Press, 1986) p. 1.

8. Ibid.

9. Ibid. p. 2.

10. Ibid. pp. 2-3.

11. Ibid. p. 3.

12. Ibid. p. 4.

13. "Literary analysis seeks to take the text on its own terms as an offer of meaning, as an exercise in creative imagination to construct a world that does not exist apart from the literary act of the text. The nuances of the the text are to simply imaginative literary moves, but are acts of world-making which create and evoke an alternative world available only through this text." Ibid. p. 5.

14. Ibid.

15. Ibid. p. 6.

16. W. Brueggemann, *Israel's Praise*, op. cit. p. 12.

17. Ibid. p. 15.

18. Ibid.

19. Ibid. p. 23.

20. Ibid.

21. Ibid. p. 24. For the author in theology we "reconstruct the religious reality which we seek to praise and obey" (p. 25).

22. Ibid. p. 12.

23. Ibid. p. 23.

24. W. Brueggemann, *The Bible Makes Sense* (Atlanta: John Knox Press, 1977) p. 150.

25. Walter Brueggemann, "A Shape for Old Testament Theology, 1: Structure Legitimation" in *The Catholic Biblical Quarterly* 47 (1985) p. 30.

26. Brueggemann writes this about process theology: "In the terms offered here, there is no doubt that God is 'in process.' It may be that such an articulation opens to an interface with so-called process theology. Perhaps so. But I am unconvinced about the enormous metaphysical superstructure of process philosophy as being useful for interpreting the Bible. It appears to me much simpler and more effective to deal with social/convenantal/personal metaphors on the

Bible's own terms. In another context I have suggested that process theology is inherently more conservative than is recognized in some quarters." In "A Shape for Old Testament Theology, II: Embrace of Pain," C.B.W. 47 (1985) p. 415.

27. Ibid. p. 412.

28. Ibid.

29. Ibid.

30. Ibid. p. 414.

31. Ibid. p. 43.

32. Ibid.

33. Ibid. p. 44.

34. Ibid.

35. W. Brueggemann, "The Rhetoric of Hurt and Hope: Ethics Odd and Crucial," op. cit. p. 73.

36. Ibid.

37. Ibid. p. 74.

38. Ibid.

39. Ibid.

40. Ibid.

41. Ibid. p. 75.

42. Ibid. p. 76.

43. Ibid. p. 77.

44. Ibid. p. 78.

45. Ibid. p. 76.

46. Ibid.

47. W. Brueggemann, "The Formfulness of Grief," *Interpretation* 31 (1979) p. 265.

48. W. Brueggemann, *The Prophetic Imagination* (Philadelphia: Fortress Press, 1985) p. 21.

49. W. Brueggemann, "From Hurt to Joy, From Death to Life," in *Interpretation* 28 (1974) p. 5.

50. "The lament in Israel is a way of asserting that the structure cannot always be legitimated, but that the pain needs also to be embraced. This pain, when brought to public speech impinges upon every structure and serves to question the legitimacy of the structure. The laments of Israel, as Westermann has seen, are not marginal, but decisive for the faith of Israel."

51. W. Brueggemann, "A Shape for Old Testament Theology, II:

Embrace of Pain," op. cit. p. 400.

52. "Israel is the community which refuses to settle for the way things are, refuses to accept the legitimated structures, refuses to accept a God who is positioned 'above the fray,' refuses to accept guilt and blame for every dysfunction. Indeed, such a theological hunch does not believe that the doctor knows best, does not believe all authority is ordained by God, does not believe city hall (in heaven or on earth) cannot be fought." Ibid. p. 402.

53. W. Brueggemann, *The Bible Makes Sense,* op. cit. p. 24.

54. W. Brueggemann, *The Message of the Psalms* (Minnesota: Augsburg Publishing House, 1984) p. 20.

55. Ibid. p. 21.

56. Ibid. p. 169.

57. Ibid. p. 170.

58. Ibid. p. 169.

59. Ibid.

60. Ibid.

61. W. Brueggemann, *Prophetic Imagination*, op. cit. p. 9.

62. Ibid. p. 14.

63. W. Brueggemann, *The Creative World Canon as a Model for Biblical Education* (Philadelphia: Fortress Press, 1982) p. 144.

64. W. Brueggemann, *David's Truth in Israel's Imagination and Memory* (Philadelphia: Fortress Press, 1985) pp. 17-18.

65. W. Brueggemann, *Israel's Praise*, op. cit. p. 139.

66. Ibid.

67. Ibid.

68. Ibid.

69. Ibid. p. 126.

70. Ibid.

71. Ibid.

2. God and Suffering: Edward Schillebeeckx

1. Edward Schillebeeckx, *Christ: The Experience of Jesus as Lord* (New York: Crossroad, 1980) p. 671.

2. Ibid. p. 672.

3. Ibid. p. 718.

4. Ibid. p. 72.

5. Ibid. p. 35.

6. Ibid.

7. Ibid. p. 811.

8. Ibid. p. 62.

9. Ibid. p. 78.

10. Edward Schillebeeckx, Interim Report on the Books *Jesus* and *Christ* (New York: Crossroad, 1981) p. 50.

11. Edward Schillebeeckx, "The Role of History in What Is Called the New Paradigm," in *Paradigm Change in Theology. A Symposium for the Future,* eds. Hans Küng and David Tracy (New York: Crossroad, 1989) p. 311.

12. Ibid. p. 312.

13 Ibid.

14. Ibid. p. 313.

15. Ibid.

16. Ibid.

17. Ibid.

18. Ibid. p. 314.

19. Edward Schillebeeckx, Interim Report, op. cit. p. 50.

20. Edward Schillebeeckx, "The Role of History in What Is Called the New Paradigm," op. cit. p. 311.

21. Edward Schillebeeckx, *Christ*, op. cit. p. 18.

22. Ibid. p. 821.

23. Edward Schillebeeckx, in *Experiment in Theology* (N.Y.: Crossroad, 1979) p. 62.

24. Edward Schillebeeckx, *Christ*, op. cit. p. 724.

25. Ibid. p. 819.

26. Ibid. p. 725.

27. Ibid.

28. Ibid.

29. Ibid. p. 726.

30. Ibid.

31. Ibid.

32. Edward Schillebeeckx, *Jesus*, op. cit. p. 618.

33. Edward Schillebeeckx, *Christ,* op. cit. p. 618.

34. Ibid. p. 695.

35. Ibid.

36. Ibid.

37. Ibid. p. 726.

38. Ibid. p. 730.

39. Ibid.

40. Ibid. p. 746.

41 Ibid. p. 768.

42. Ibid. p. 729.

43. Ibid. p. 801.

44. Ibid. p. 811.

45. Ibid. p. 794.

46. Ibid.

47. Ibid. p. 695.

48. Ibid. p. 794.

49. Ibid.

50. Ibid. p. 795.

51. Ibid. p. 640.

52. Ibid. p. 834.

53. Ibid.

54. Ibid. p. 820.

55. Ibid. p. 729.

56. Edward Schillebeeckx, *Jesus,* op. cit. p. 643.

57. Edward Schillebeeckx, *Christ,* op. cit. p. 819.

58. Edward Schillebeeckx, *God Among Us. The Gospel Proclaimed* (New York: Crossroad, 1983) p. 253.

59. Edward Schillebeeckx, *Jesus,* op. cit. p. 623.

60. Edward Schillebeeckx, "The Role of History in What Is Called the New Paradigm," in *Paradigm Change in Theology: A Symposium for the Future*, op. cit. p. 317.

61. Edward Schillebeeckx, *Christ,* op. cit. p. 814.

62. Ibid. p. 819.

63. Ibid. p. 80.

64. Ibid. p. 817.

65. Ibid. p. 530.

66. Edward Schillebeeckx, *Jesus: An Experiment in Christology* (New York: Crossroad, 1978) p. 621.

67. Ibid.

68. Edward Schillebeeckx, *Christ,* op. cit. p. 622.

69. Edward Schillebeeckx, *Jesus,* op. cit. p. 818.

70. Ibid. p. 24.

71. Ibid. p. 622.

72. Ibid. pp. 35–36.

73. Ibid. p. 34.

74. Edward Schillebeeckx, *Christ,* op. cit. p. 60.

75. Edward Schillebeeckx, *Jesus*, op. cit. p. 791.

3. The Suffering of God in the Theology of Jürgen Moltmann

1. Jürgen Moltmann, Foreword in Richard, Bauckham, Moltmann, *Messianic Theology in the Making* (London: Marshall Pickering, 1987) p. viii.

2. J. Moltmann, *The Way of Jesus Christ. Christology in Messianic Dimensions* (San Francisco: Harper Press, 1989) p. 152.

3. Cf. Jürgen Moltmann, "Antwort auf die Kritik an *Der Gekreuzigte Gott,*" in *Diskussion uber Jürgen Moltmanns Buch "Der Gekreuzigte Gott," herausgegeben und eingeleitet von Michael Welker* (München: Chr. Kaiser, 1979) p. 168.

4. Cf. Jürgen Moltmann, "Der gekreuzigte Gott, neuzeitliche Gottesfrage und trinitarische Gottesgeschicte," *Concilium* 8 (1972) p. 408.

5. Jürgen Moltmann, *Religion, Revolution and the Future* (New York: Charles Scribner's Sons, 1968) p. 206.

6. Jürgen Moltmann, *The Crucified God: The Cross as the Foundation and Criticism of Christian Theology,* trans. R.A. Wilson and J. Bowden (London: SCM Press, 1974) p. 153.

7. Ibid. p. 253

8. Ibid.

9. Ibid.

10. J. Moltmann, *The Experiment of Hope*, ed. and trans. M.D. Meeks (London: SCM Press, 1975) p. 96.

11. J. Moltmann, *The Church in the Power of the Spirit: A Contribution to Messianic Ecclesiology,* trans. M. Kohl (London: SCM Press, 1977) p. 167.

12. "Today people prefer rather to overlook the suffering which is part of every great passion. To be painlessly happy, and to conquer every form of suffering, is part of the dream of modern society. But since the dream is unattainable, people anaesthetize pain, and suppress suffering, and by so doing rob themselves of the passion for life. But

life without passion is poverty-stricken. Life without the preparedness for suffering is superficial. The fear of passion has to be surmounted just as much as the fear of suffering if life is to be really lived and affirmed to the point of death." In J. Moltmann, *The Way of Jesus Christ,* op. cit. p. 151.

13. Ibid. p. 167.

14. J. Moltmann, *The Crucified God*, op. cit. p. 7.

15. Ibid. p. 212.

16. Ibid. p. 64.

17. Ibid. p. 212.

18. Ibid. p. 69.

19. The apathetic God of theism is described by Moltmann in the following fashion: "God is good and cannot be the cause of evil. God is perfect and thus has no needs. God is sufficient and thus needs neither love nor hate. Nothing can befall him that would make him suffer. He knows neither wrath nor grace. God is totally free. Therefore, since Aristotle, it has been said: *theos apathes.* The wise man's moral ideal is to become similar to God and to share in his domain. The wise man must overcome his drives and needs and lead a life free from trouble and fear, from wrath and love, in short, an apathetic life." In J. Moltmann, *The Experiment of Hope,* op. cit. pp. 73–74.

20. J. Moltmann, "Political Theology" in *Theology Today* 28 (1971) p. 8.

21. J. Moltmann, *Religion, Revolution and the Future*, M.D. Meeks, trans. (New York: Charles Scribner's Sons, 1969).

22. "Political theology would like to try to interpret the dangerous memory of the message of Christ within the conditions of contemporary society in order to free man practically from the coercions of this society and to prepare the way for the eschatological freedom of the new man." In J. Moltmann, "Political Theology," op. cit. p. 8.

23. Influenced by Hegel, Moltmann writes: "If the one profaned with crucifixion by the authority of the states is the Christ of God, then what is lowest in the political imagination is changed into what is highest. What the state had considered the deepest humiliation, namely the cross, bears the highest dignity. When the cross is raised as a standard, whose political content is the Kingdom of God, then the life

of the state is deprived of its inner disposition, that is, religion." Ibid. p. 16.

24. "Out of the mere negation elements, no definition of positive reality emerges. For this reason eschatology cannot be developed only as negative theology. The negation of negative elements must have its basis in a hidden anticipation of positive reality, otherwise the negation would not be experienced and criticized as such. It is the experience of divine promissory history ever striving for fulfillment that Biblical eschatology anchors the negation of negative elements." In J. Moltmann, "Creation and Redemption" in R.W. McKinney, ed., *Creation, Christ and Culture* (Edinburgh, Scotland: T. & T. Clark, 1976) p. 229.

25. J. Moltmann, *On Human Dignity: Political Theology and Ethics,* trans. M.D. Meeks (London: SCM Press, 1984) p. 109.

26. J. Moltmann, "Political Theology," op. cit. p. 23.

27. J. Moltmann, *On Human Dignity*, op. cit. p. 103.

28. J. Moltmann, *The Crucified God*, op. cit. p. 46.

29. Ibid. p. 246.

30. Ibid.

31. J. Moltmann, *The Way of Jesus Christ,* op. cit. p. 173.

32. Ibid. p. 156

33. Ibid.

34. Ibid. p. 174.

35. "*God himself was in Christ* (II Cor. 5. 19). Jesus' weakness was God's weakness too; Jesus' suffering was God's suffering; Jesus' death also meant his death for God his Father: 'I am in the Father and the Father is in me,' says the Johannine Christ. By virtue of this mutual indwelling (perichoresis) of the Father and the Son, Jesus' sufferings are divine sufferings, and God's love is love that is able to suffer and is prepared to suffer. The power of the divine Spirit in Jesus is transformed from an active power that works wonders to a suffering power that endures wounds." Ibid. p. 177.

36. Ibid. p. 178.

37. Ibid.

38. "God experiences history in order to affect history. He goes out of himself in order to gather into himself. He is vulnerable, takes suffering and death on himself in order to heal, to liberate and to confer new life. The history of God's suffering in the passion of the Son and

the sighings of the Spirit serves the history of God's joy in the Spirit and his completed felicity at the end. That is the ultimate goal of God's history of suffering in the world. But once the joy of union is complete the history of suffering does not become obsolete and a thing of the past. As suffering that has been endured, and which has brought about liberation, eternal life and union, it remains the ground of eternal joy in the salvation of God and his new creation." In J. Moltmann, *The Church in the Power of the Spirit,* op.cit. p. 64.

39. J. Moltmann,, *The Crucified God,* op. cit. p. 222.

40. "The 'bifurcation' in God must contain the whole uproar of history within itself. Men must be able to recognize rejection, the curse, and final nothingness in it.... The concrete 'history of God' in the death of Jesus on the cross on Golgotha therefore contains within itself all the depths and abysses of human history and therefore can be understood as the history of history. All human history, however much it may be determined by guilt and death, is taken up into this 'history of God,' i.e., into the Trinity, and integrated into the future of the 'history of God.' There is no suffering which in this history is not God's suffering; no death which has not been God's death in the history of Golgotha." Ibid. p. 246.

41. Jürgen Moltmann, "The Motherly Father. Is Trinitarian Patricompassionism Replacing Theological Patriarchalism?" *Concilum* 143 *God as Father,* ed J. B. Metz and E. Schillebeeckx (1981) p. 54.

42. Jürgen Moltmann, *The Crucified God,* op. cit. p. 252.

43. Ibid. p. 277

44. "Anyone who 'has compassion' participates in the suffering of the other, takes another person's suffering on himself, suffers for others by entering into community with them and bearing their burdens. This suffering in solidarity, vicarious suffering which in its vicariousness saves, is the suffering of God. If we are to understand its full scope, we have to grasp it in trinitarian terms. It is the suffering of the Creator who preserves the world and endures its conflicts and contradictions, in order to sustain it in life. It is the special suffering of Christ, who, in his community with us and his self-giving for us, suffers the pains of redemption. It is, finally, the suffering of God's Spirit in the birth-pangs of the new creation." In Jürgen Moltmann, *The Way of Jesus Christ,* op. cit. p. 178.

45. Jürgen Moltmann, "The Diaconal Church in the Context of

the Kingdom of God," in *Hope for the Church. Moltmann in Dialogue with Practical Theology,* ed. and trans. by Theodore Runyon (Nashville: Abingdon, 1979) p. 29.

46. Ibid.

47. Jürgen Moltmann, *The Open Church: Invitation to the Messianic Lifestyle,* trans. M.D. Meeks (London: SCM Press, 1978) p. 93.

48. "It is only the person who knows loneliness and does not flee from it who can hold community with the lonely. It is only the person who knows the frontier where all human help fails who can stand by the helpless. It is only the person who knows the guilt which no one can make good who can remain beside the guilty. It is only the person who has made dying a part of his life and no longer represses it who can accompany the dying.

Solidarity in the depths is the community of the suffering, the guilty and those who mourn. They can no longer help themselves and support one another simply through that very fact. I believe that no fellowship is more profound and no sympathy communicates a deeper happiness than this solidarity in the depths." In Jürgen Moltmann, *The Power of the Powerless,* trans. M. Kohl (London: SCM Press, 1983) p. 110.

49. Jürgen Moltmann, *The Way of Jesus Christ,* op. cit. p. 153.

50. Ibid. p. 70.

51. Ibid. p. 55.

52. "Nor can one follow Jürgen Moltmann in solving the problem of suffering by 'eternalizing' suffering in God, in the opinion that in the last resort this gives suffering some splendour. According to Moltmann, Jesus not only shows solidarity 'with publicans and sinners,' with the outcast and those who are everywhere excluded; not only has God himself identified him with the outcast; no, God himself has cast him out as a sacrifice for our sins. The difficulty in this conception is that it ascribes to God what has in fact been done to Jesus by the history of human injustice. Hence I think that in soteriology or the doctrine of redemption we are on a false trail, despite the deep and correct insight here that God is the great fellow-sufferer, who is concerned for our history." In E. Schillebeeckx, *Christ, the Experience of Jesus as Lord* (New York: Crossroad, 1980) p. 728.

53. Dorothy Soelle, *Suffering* (Philadelphia: Fortress Press, 1975) p. 27.

54. Jürgen Moltmann, *The Way of Jesus Christ,* op. cit. p. 178.

55. Ibid. p. 175.

56. Ibid. p. 177.

57. Jürgen Moltmann, *The Experiment of Hope,* op. cit. pp. 7–8.

58. Jürgen Moltmann, *Theology of Play,* Reinhard Ulrich, trans. (New York: Harper & Row, 1972) p. 71.

4. Theology and Suffering After the End of Idealism: Johannes B. Metz

1. Johannes B. Metz, "Theology in the New Paradigm," in *Paradigm Change in Theology. A Symposium for the Future,* Hans Küng and David Tracy, eds. (New York: Crossroad, 1989) p. 362.

2. Johannes B. Metz, "The Future in the Memory of Suffering," in *Concilium* 76 (1972) p. 16.

3. Ibid.

4. Ibid.

5.Ibid. p. 17.

6. Ibid.

7. J.B. Metz, "Theology in the New Paradigm," op. cit. p. 362: "And this theology is political theology. Its hermeneutics is a political hermeneutics, a hermeneutics in the awareness of danger. It criticizes the high degree of apathy in theological idealism, and its defective sensibility for the interruptive character of historical and political catastrophes."

8. Ibid. pp. 362–363.

9. Ibid. p. 363: "It begins with the question about the deliverance of those who have suffered unjustly, the victims of our history and the defeated. It continually brings this question anew into the political awareness as indictment, and expounds the concept of a strict universal solidarity, which also includes the dead, as a practical and political idea, on which the fate of human beings as clear and evident subjects depends."

10. J.B. Metz, *Faith in History and Society. Toward a Practical Fundamental Theology,* trans. by David Smith (New York: Crossroad, 1990) p. 152.

11. Ibid. p. 127.

12. Here J.B. Metz, is under the influence of Walter Benjamin.

13. J.B. Metz, *Faith in History and Society,* op. cit. p. 108.

14. J.B. Metz, *Theology of the World,* trans. by William Glen-Doepel (New York: Herder and Herder, 1969) pp. 113–114.

15. J.B. Metz, "The Future in the Memory of Suffering," op. cit. p. 123.

16. Ibid.

17. See J.B. Metz, *Faith in History and Society,* op. cit. pp. 46–47.

18. Ibid. p. 92.

19. Ibid.

20. Ibid. p. 183.

21. Ibid. p. 195.

22. J.B. Metz, "The Future in the Memory of Suffering," op. cit. p. 14.

23. Ibid.

24. J.B. Metz, "Redemption and Emancipation" in *Cross Currents* 27 (1977) p. 333.

25. J.B. Metz, "A Short Apology of Narrative," in *Concilium* 85 (1973) p. 88.

26. J.B. Metz, *Faith in History and Society,* op. cit. p. 213.

27. Ibid. p. 211.

28. Rebecca Chopp, *The Praxis of Suffering. An Interpretation of Liberation and Political Theologies* (Maryknoll: Orbis Books, 1986) p. 75.

29. J.B. Metz, *Faith in History and Society,* op. cit. p. 232.

30. Ibid.

31. Ibid. p. 229.

32. Ibid.

33. Ibid.

34. Gabriel Marcel, *The Mystery of Being* (Chicago: Regency Press, 1951) p. 28.

35. J.B. Metz, *Faith in History and Society,* op. cit. pp. 57-58.

36. Ibid. pp. 89–90.

37. J.B. Metz, *The Emergent Church,* trans. Peter Mann (New York: Crossroad, 1981) p. 150.

38. J.B. Metz, *Faith in History and Society,* op. cit. p. 73.

39. Ibid. p. 112.

40. E. Schillebeeckx, *Christ: The Experience of Jesus as Lord* (New York: Seabury Press, 1980) p. 755.

5. Suffering from a Feminist Perspective: Dorothy Soelle

1. Dorothy Soelle, *Suffering,* trans. Everett R. Kalin (Philadelphia: Fortress Press, 1975).

2. Dorothy Soelle, *Christ the Representative: An Essay in Theology After the "Death of God,"* trans. David Lewis (Philadelphia: Fortress Press, 1967) p. 10.

3. Dorothy Soelle, *The Strength of the Weak: Toward A Christian Feminist Identity,* trans. Robert and Rita Kimber (Philadelphia: The Westminster Press, 1984) p. 91.

4. Ibid.

5. Ibid. p. 90.

6. Ibid.

7. Ibid p. 91.

8. Dorothy Soelle, *Suffering,* op. cit. p. 11.

9. Dorothy Soelle, *The Strength of the Weak,* op. cit. p. 96.

10. Ibid.

11. Again Soelle writes, "The most important criticisms that an incipient feminist theology has to make of the current dominant theology are directed against these phallocratic fantasies, against the accumulation of power and the worship of power. Why should we honor and love a being that does not transcend but only reaffirms the moral level of our present male-dominated culture?" Ibid. p. 97.

12. Ibid. p. 98.

13. Dorothy Soelle, *Thinking About God. An Introduction to Theology* (Philadelphia: Trinity Press, International, 1990) p. 70.

14. Ibid. p. 71.

15. Dorothy Soelle, *Suffering,* op. cit. p. 2.

16. Dorothy Soelle, *Political Theology*, trans. John Shelley (Philadelphia: Fortress Press, 1974) p. 67.

17. Ibid. p. 59.

18. Ibid. p. 62.

19. Dorothy Soelle, *Christ the Representative,* op. cit. p. 9.

20. Dorothy Soelle, *Suffering,* op. cit. p. 39.

21. Ibid. p. 4.

22. Ibid. p. 39.

23. Dorothy Soelle, *The Strength of the Weak,* op. cit. p. 24.

24. Ibid. p. 25.

25. Dorothy Soelle, *Suffering,* op. cit. p. 67.

26. Ibid. p. 75.

27. Ibid. p. 78.

28. Ibid.

29. Ibid. p. 8.

30. Ibid. p. 6.

31. Dorothy Soelle, *The Strength of the Weak,* op. cit. p. 96.

32. Ibid. p. 98.

33. Ibid.

34. "In the understanding of scholastic theology God exists *a se*; he derives himself from himself and not from another. Only God has the privilege of being *a se:* it ensures his infinite superiority. God could create the world, but he could also have left it alone. God is not concerned with those who love him." In Dorothy Soelle, *Thinking About God,* op. cit. p. 781.

35. "The theological presumption of God's absolute otherness has consequences in three dimensions: for God, for the earth, and for the human being. If God is absolutely transcendent, then God is rendered invisible as the Creator for whom there can be no human analogies. There is no interaction between such a creator and us. He creates the world out of his free will; he does not need to create it. His creation is an act of absolute freedom. Absolute transcendence literally means unrelatedness. Classical theology viewed the opposite of unrelatedness—relationality—as the weakness of the being bound through passion and suffering to other beings. Hence, the transcendent God in his absolute freedom is a projection of the patriarchal world view and its ideal of the independent king, warrior, or hero." In Dorothy Soelle and Shirley Cloyes, *To Work and to Love: A Theology of Creation* (Philadelphia: Fortress Press, 1984) p. 14.

36. Dorothy Soelle, *Suffering,* op. cit. p. 42.

37. Ibid. p. 17.

38. Ibid. p. 19.

39. Ibid. p. 24.

40. Ibid. p. 42.

41. Ibid. p. 43.

42 Ibid. p. 143.

43. Ibid. p. 142.

44. Ibid. p. 143.

45. Ibid.

46. Dorothy Soelle, *The Strength of the Weak,* op. cit. p. 29.

47. Cf. Dorothy Soelle, *Suffering,* op. cit. pp. 26-28.

48. Dorothy Soelle, *Beyond Mere Dialogue: On Being Christian and Socialist* (Detroit: Christians for Socialism, 1978) p. 38.

49. Dorothy Soelle, *Beyond Mere Obedience,* trans. Lawrence W. Denel (New York: The Pilgrim Press, 1982) p. xix.

50. Dorothy Soelle, *Thinking About God,* op. cit. p. 183.

51. Ibid. pp. 187–188.

52. Ibid. p. 191.

53. Ibid. p. 192.

54. Ibid.

55. Ibid. p. 188.

56. "How can we distinguish good power, the power of life, from evil power, the power to dominate? This question is central for a feminist and thus humane way of thinking. The most important criterion for answering it is that good power is shared power, power which distributes itself, which involves others, which grows through dispersion and does not become less. In this sense the resurrection of Christ is a tremendous distribution of power. The women who were the first to experience it were given a share in the power of life. It was the tremendous certainty of God which now entered their life." Ibid.

57. Ibid. p. 189.

58. Dorothy Soelle, "God's Pain and Our Pain" in *The Future of Liberation Theology,* eds. Marc Ellis and Otto Maduro (Maryknoll: Orbis Books, 1989) p. 332.

59. Ibid.

60. Dorothy Soelle, *Suffering,* op. cit. p. 45.

61. "The story also has been misunderstood in a second way, from a dogmatic perspective that views the suffering and death of Jesus as unique. One perhaps stresses in such a case that Jesus suffered more than and differently from other martyrs because he saw himself as cast out and cursed, and God was inaccessible to him as he suffered. Jesus' distinctiveness, his incomparability, since they are not to be

rescued by reference to an apathy that would make him too lofty to suffer, are here supposed to be kept at least in the *pathein*, the suffering. This way of stating that issue, that in a world of immeasurable suffering wants to isolate Jesus' suffering and make it something that outweighs the rest in order to be able to understand it as unique, is rather macabre. It is not in Jesus' interest to have suffered 'the most.' " Ibid. p. 81.

62. Ibid. p. 87.
63. Ibid. p. 145.
64. Ibid. p. 70.
65. Ibid. p. 88.
66. Ibid. p. 92.
67. Ibid. p. 94.
68. Ibid. p. 127.
69. Dorothy Soelle, *Thinking About God,* op. cit. p. 132.
70. Ibid. p. 133.
71. Ibid. p. 134.

6. Liberation Theology and Suffering:
The Theology of Gustavo Gutierrez

1. Jon Sobrino, "Theology in a Suffering World: Theology as *Intellectus Amoris,"* in *Pluralism and Oppression, Theology in World Perspective,* ed. Paul Knitten. The Annual Publications of the College Theology Society, vol. 34 (Lanham: University Press of America, 1988) p. 159.
2. Ibid.
3. Ibid.
4. Ibid.
5. Ibid. p. 156.
6. Ibid.
7. Ibid. p. 160.
8. Ibid.
9. Ibid. p. 156.
10. Ibid. p. 157.
11. Ibid.
12. Ibid. p. 168.
13. Ibid.

14. Ibid. p. 167.

15. Peter Henriot, S.J., *Opting for the Poor: A Challenge for North Americans* (Washington, D.C.: Center for Concern, 1990) pp. 24–25.

16. Desmond Tutu, "The Theology of Liberation in Africa," in Kofi Appiah-Kubi and Sergio Torres, eds., *African Theology en Route: Papers from the Pan-African Conference of Third World Theologians, December 17–23, 1977, Accra, Ghana* (Maryknoll: Orbis, 1979) p. 163.

17. Gustavo Gutierrez, *On Job, God-Talk and the Suffering of the Innocent* (Maryknoll: Orbis Books, 1987).

18. Ibid. xiv–xv.

19. Ibid. xv.

20. Gutierrez describes this "irruption" in the following way: "The most recent years of Latin American history have been characterized by the discovery of the real-life world of the 'other,' of the poor and the exploited and their compelling needs. In a social order fashioned economically, politically, and ideologically by a few for their own benefit, the 'other side' has begun to make its voice heard. The lower classes of the populace, forced to live on the margins of society and oppressed since time immemorial, are beginning to speak for themselves more and more rather than relying on intermediaries. They have discovered themselves once again, and they now want the existing system to take note of their disturbing presence. They are less and less willing to be the passive objects of demagogic manipulation and social or charitable welfare in varied disguises. They want to be the active subjects of their own history and to forge a radically different society." In Gustavo Gutierrez, "Liberating Praxis and Christian Faith," *Frontiers of Theology in Latin America,* ed. Rosino Gibellini, trans. John Drury (Maryknoll: Orbis Books, 1974) p. 1.

21. Gustavo Gutierrez, *We Drink from Our Own Wells: The Spiritual Journey of a People,* trans. Matthew J. O'Connell (Maryknoll: Orbis Books; Melbourne: Dove Communications, 1984) p. 136.

22. Gustavo Gutierrez, *A Theology of Liberation History, Politics, and Salvation,* trans. Sister Chridan Inda and John Eagleson (Maryknoll: Orbis Press, 1971) p. 102.

23. Ibid. p. 164.

24. Ibid. p. 165.

25. Ibid.

26. Ibid. p. 168.

27. Ibid.

28. Ibid. p. 170.

29. Ibid. p. 172.

30. Ibid.

31. Ibid. p. 173.

32. G. Gutierrez, *The Power of the Poor in History: Selected Works,* trans. Robert R. Barr (Maryknoll: Orbis Books, 1983) p. 85.

33. G. Gutierrez, *The Book of Job,* op. cit. pp. 12–13.

34. Ibid. xv.

35. G. Gutierrez, "Liberating Praxis and the Christian Faith," op. cit. p. 8.

36. G. Gutierrez, *The Power of the Poor,* op. cit. p. 129.

37. G. Gutierrez, "Freedom and Salvation. A Political Problem," in *Liberation and Change* by G. Gutierrez and Richard Shaull (Atlanta: John Knox Press, 1977) p. 88.

38. Ibid. p. 82: "Theology, in this context, will be a critical reflection on the historical praxis when confronted with the Word of the Lord lived and accepted in faith; this faith comes to us through multiple and, at times, ambiguous historical meditations which we make and discover every day. Theology will be a reflection in and on faith as a liberating praxis. the understanding of faith will proceed from an option and a commitment. This understanding will start with a real and effective solidarity with discriminated races, despised cultures, and exploited classes and from their very world and atmosphere. This reflection starts from a commitment to create a just, fraternal society, and must contribute to make it more meaningful, radical, and universal. This theological process becomes truth when it is embodied in the process of liberation."

39. G. Gutierrez, *On Job,* op. cit. p. 11.

40. Ibid. p. 102.

41. Ibid. p. 103.

42. Ibid. p. 12.

43. Ibid. p. 16.

44. Ibid. p. 101.

45. G. Gutierrez, *The Power of the Poor,* op. cit. p. 230.

46. Ibid. pp. 104–105.

47. G. Gutierrez, "Terrorism, Liberation, and Sexuality," in *The Witness,* April 1977, p. 10.

48. G. Gutierrez, *A Theology of Liberation*, op. cit. p. 67.

49. Ibid. p. 238.

50. Ibid. p. 216.

51. Ibid. p. 233.

52. José Comblin, *The Church and the National Security State* (Maryknoll: Orbis, 1979) p. 6.

53. G. Gutierrez, *On the Book of Job,* op. cit. p. 49.

54. Ibid. pp. 87–88.

55. Ibid. p. 88.

56. Ibid. p. 89.

57. Ibid. p. 94.

58. Ibid. p. xiv: "The time of silence is the time of loving encounter with God and of prayer and commitment; it is a time of 'staying with him' (John 1:39). As the experience of human love shows us, in this kind of encounter we enter depths and regions that are ineffable. When words do not suffice, when they are incapable of communicating what is experienced at the affective level, then we are fully engaged in loving. And when words are incapable of showing forth our experience, we fall back on symbols, which are another way of remaining silent. For when we use a symbol, we do not speak; we let an object or gesture speak for us. This is precisely how we proceed in the liturgy; symbolic language—the language of love that transcends words."

59. Ibid. p. 96: "The world of unmerited love is not a place dominated by the arbitrary or the superfluous. Without the prophetic dimension the language of contemplation is in danger of having no grip on the history in which God acts and in which we meet God. Without the mystical dimension the language of prophecy can narrow its vision and weaken its perception of the God who makes all things new (Rev. 21:5). Each undergoes a distortion that isolates it and renders it inauthentic."

60. Ibid. p. 96: "The journey of prophecy and the journey of contemplation are precisely that—a journey. The road must be traveled in freedom without turning from it because of its pitfalls, and without pretending ignorance of its ever new forms, for unjust human suffering

continues to be heartrending and insatiable; it continually raises new questions and causes new dilemmas. It never ends; neither does protest, after the manner of Job. Although the way of talking about God has become clearer, it continues to be mysterious, as awesome and as alluring as ever."

61. Ibid. p. 97.

62. Ibid. p. 100.

63. Ibid. p. 101.

64. Cf. G. Gutierrez, "Two Theological Perspectives," op. cit. p. 25.

7. Ethics and Suffering: Stanley Hauerwas

1. Stanley Hauerwas, *Suffering Presence* (Notre Dame: University of Note Dame Press, 1986) p. 25.

2. Ibid.

3. Stanley Hauerwas, *Vision and Virtue. Essays in Christian Ethical Reflection* (Notre Dame: Fides Publishers, Inc., 1974) p. 36.

4. Stanley Hauerwas, *Truthfulness and Tragedy, Further Investigations in Christian Ethics* (Notre Dame: University of Notre Dame Press, 1977).

5. Stanley Hauerwas, *Naming the Silences. God, Medicine and the Problem of Suffering* (Grand Rapids: William Eerdmans Publishing Co., 1990) p. 67.

6. "Christianity offers a narrative about God's relationship to creation that gives us the means to recognize we are God's creatures. Thus it is certainly true that the God we find in the story of Jesus is the same God we find in creation—namely, the God who wills us to share in his life. We have a saving God, and we are saved by being invited to share in the work of the kingdom through the history God has created in Israel and the work of Jesus. Such a history completes our nature as well as our particular history by placing us within an adventure which we claim is nothing less than God's purpose for all of creation." In Stanley Hauerwas, *The Peaceable Kingdom. A Primer in Christian Ethics* (Notre Dame: University of Notre Dame Press, 1983) p. 62.

7. "By the phrase 'the significance of narrative,' we mean to call attention to three points: (1) that character and moral notions only take on meaning in a narrative; (2) that narrative and explanation stand

in an intimate relationship, and therefore moral disagreements involve rival histories of explanations; and (3) that the standard account of moral objectivity is the obverse of existentialist ethics since the latter assumes that the failure of secure moral objectivity implies that all moral judgements must be subjective or arbitrary." In Stanley Hauerwas and Gregory Jones, *Why Narrative? Readings in Narrative Theology* (Grand Rapids: W.B. Eerdmans, 1989) p. 159.

8. Ibid. p. 185.

9. Stanley Hauerwas, *Peaceable Kingdom,* op. cit. p. 60.

10. Ibid. p. 55.

11. Ibid. p. 54.

12. From within the Kantian perspective, Hauerwas writes about contemporary ethics: "Modern people like to think of themselves as independent, reasoning, and acting agents. Morality is an individual, personal determination of the facts, not a matter of experience, tradition, training, or community. Anybody, regardless of education or family background, can be just as moral as any other person— provided that the person acts on the basis of some general, universally applicable notion of what is right. The basis for right action is the general perspective of almost anybody." In Stanley Hauerwas and William H. Willimon, *Resident Aliens* (Nashville: Abingdon Press, 1989) p. 98.

13. Ibid.

14. Stanley Hauerwas, *The Peaceable Kingdom,* op. cit. p. 68.

15. Ibid. p. 69.

16. Ibid. p. 24.

17. Ibid. p. 25.

18. Ibid. p. 26.

19. Ibid. p. 29.

20. Ibid.

21. Stanley Hauerwas, *Vision and Virtue,* op. cit. p. 242.

22. Ibid.

23. Ibid. p. 243.

24. Ibid. p. 244.

25. Ibid. p. 245.

26. Ibid.

27. Stanley Hauerwas, *Resident Aliens,* op. cit. p. 39.

28. Stanley Hauerwas, *The Peaceable Kingdom,* op. cit. p. 63.

29. Stanley Hauerwas, *Against the Nations,* op. cit. p. 63.

30. Ibid. p. 41.

31. Ibid. p. 42.

32. Ibid. p. 43.

33. Ibid. p. 45.

34. Stanley Hauerwas, *Resident Aliens,* op. cit.

35. Stanley Hauerwas, *Character and the Christian Life: A Study in Theological Ethics* (San Antonio: Trinity University Press, 1975) p. 11.

36. Stanley Hauerwas, *A Community of Character: Toward a Constructive Christian Social Ethic* (Notre Dame: University of Notre Dame Press, 1981) p. 66.

37. Ibid. p. 30.

38. Stanley Hauerwas, *Character and the Christian Life,* op. cit. p. 230.

39. Ibid.

40. Ibid.

41. Ibid.

42. Ibid.

43. Ibid. p. 231.

44. Ibid.

45. Ibid. p. 233.

46. Stanley Hauerwas, *Naming the Silences,* op. cit. p. x.

47. Ibid. p. ix.

48. Ibid. p. x.

49. Ibid.

50. Ibid. p. xi.

51. Ibid.

52. Stanley Hauerwas, *Suffering Presence. Theological Reflections on Medicine, the Mentally Handicapped, and the Church* (Notre Dame: Notre Dame University Press, 1986) p. 28.

53. Ibid. p. 165; cf. also p. 29.

54. Ibid. p. 28.

55. Ibid. p. 165.

56. Ibid.

57. Ibid.

58. Ibid. pp. 165–166.

59. Ibid. p. 166.

60. Ibid.

61. Ibid.

62. Ibid.

63. Ibid. p. 175.

64. Ibid. p. 167.

65. Ibid. p. 168.

66. Ibid. p. 167.

67. Ibid.

68. Ibid. p. 168.

69. Ibid. p. 169.

70. Ibid.

71. Ibid. p. 167.

72. Ibid. p. 168.

73. Stanley Hauerwas, *Naming the Silences,* op. cit. p. 56.

74. Ibid. pp. 78–79.

75. Ibid. p. 79.

76. "We are able to do so because we know that the God who has made our life possible is not a God merely of goodness and power, but the God whom we find manifested in the calling of Israel and the life, cross, and resurrection of Jesus of Nazareth. The God who calls us to service through worship is not a God who insures that our lives will not be disturbed; indeed, if we are faithful, we had better expect to experience a great deal of unrest. This may not be the God we want, but at least it is a God whose very complexity is so fascinating that our attention is captivated by the wonder of the life God has given us—a life that includes pain and suffering that seem to have no point." Ibid. p. 82.

77. Stanley Hauerwas, *Suffering Presence,* op. cit. p. 31.

78. Stanley Hauerwas, *Naming the Silences,* op. cit. p. 58.

79. Stanley Hauerwas, *Suffering Presence,* op. cit. p. 178.

80. Ibid. p. 179.

81. Stanley Hauerwas, *Vision and Virtue,* op. cit. p. 189.

82. Stanley Hauerwas, *Truthfulness and Tragedy,* op. cit. p. 138.

83. Ibid.

84. Stanley Hauerwas, *Resident Aliens,* op. cit. p. 47.

85. Stanley Hauerwas, *Naming the Silences,* op. cit. pp. 84–85.

86. Ibid. p. 85.

87. Ibid. p. 86.

88. "When Christians try to explain all suffering in and of itself having theological significance we end up vacating the cross of its significance because we fail to remember that what is important about the cross is who was crucified there. Moreover such accounts of suffering tempt us to masochistic accounts of the Christian life that cannot help but belie the joy characteristic of the Christian orientation." Ibid.

89. "For example, the very willingness of those who are suffering from illness to be in the presence of the well is a form of service. Suffering and pain make us vulnerable, and often we try to protect ourselves by attempting to be 'self-sufficient.' The willingness to be present as well as to accept the assistance of others when we need help is a gift we give one another. The trick, of course, is to be the kind of community in which such a gift does not become the occasion for manipulating each other, for trying to obtain through our weakness what we cannot get others to give us voluntarily." In Stanley Hauerwas, *Naming the Silences,* op. cit. p. 89.

90. "Suffering is often regarded as a threat to autonomy, but if I have been right, we only gain autonomy by our willingness to make suffering our own through its incorporation into our moral projects. For autonomy is a correlative of our having a narrative through which we can make our suffering our own. Insofar as medicine denies us our suffering, rather than being a way to regain autonomy, it can be a threat or temptation to lose our autonomy." Ibid. p. 34.

91. Ibid. pp. 82–83.

92. Ibid. p. 50.

93. James M. Gustafson, "The Sectarian Temptation: Reflections on Theology, the Church and the University" in *CTSA Proceedings,* Vol. 40 (1985) p. 94.

Conclusion

1. Ernest Becker, *The Denial of Death* (New York: the Free Press, 1973) p. 284.

2. Jon Sobrino writes: "Stated simply, the task of theology today, either in the First or Third Worlds, cannot be carried out if the massive, cruel, and mounting suffering that pervades our world is ignored. If a theology closes its eyes to suffering because such

suffering is not occurring massively in 'its' world, that theology would disassociate itself from the real historical humanity in which we all live and which, theologically, is God's own creation. *In a world of suffering,* therefore, what is at stake is the humanity of human beings and the faith of believers. And for these two foundational reasons, the relevance and the credibility of theology is also at stake." In "Theology in a Suffering World: Theology as *Intellectus Amoris,*" in *Pluralism and Oppression,* Paul F. Knitter, ed., The Annual Publication of the College Theological Society (1988) Vol. 34 (Lanham: University Press of America, 1991).

3. "The obvious question arises: if God is and if he is truly a God of human beings, what is the source of evil, of unmerited suffering in all its varied forms? Why and for what purpose is there exploitation and oppression, guilt, anxiety, sickness and death, persecution and rejection? Not least of all: why and for what purpose is the suffering of children who are not only personally innocent but are exposed to suffering without any possible protection? These experiences of unmerited and unjust suffering are existentially a much stronger argument against faith in God than are all the epistemological and scientific arguments, all the arguments used by critics of religion and ideology, all the other philosophical arguments of whatever kind. These experiences are in fact the rock on which atheism stands." In E. Schillebeeckx, *Jesus: An Experiment in Christology* (New York: The Seabury Press, 1979) pp. 158–159.

4. "If the process of deliverance had not reached this point, Job would have retained a bit of the theology of retribution and with it, a myopic view of God. The irony in God's speeches is, as it were, the scalpel that cuts into Job's wounded flesh and makes it impossible for the evil to remain and put forth new shoots. This critical juncture has been difficult and painful, but the result is worth the suffering. . . . Job still has many questions, but the unknown is no longer a monster that threatens to devour everything, including his few and fragile certainties. The beast that is his ignorance has not vanished, but like Behemoth and Leviathan, it is under control because of what he now knows about God and God's love." In G. Gutierrez, *On Job: God-Talk and the Suffering of the Innocent* (Maryknoll: Orbis, 1987) p. 91.

5. John Paul II, "The Christian Meaning of Human Suffering," in *Origins* Feb. 23, 1989, Vol. 13, no. 37, p. 618.

6. Joanne Carlson Brown/Rebecca Parker, "For God So Loved the World?" in *Christianity, Patriarchy, and Abuse,* Joanne Carlson Brown, ed. (New York: Pilgrim Press, 1989) p. 26.

7. Mary Daly, *Beyond God the Father* (Boston: Beacon Press, 1973) p. 77.

8. As Daniel Day Williams affirms, "God does suffer as he participates in the ongoing life of the society of being. His sharing in the world's suffering is the supreme instance of knowing, accepting, and transforming in love the suffering which arises in the world. I am affirming the doctrine of the divine sensitivity. Without it I can make no sense of the being of God. Sensitive participation in this world means suffering, or else our human experience is completely irrelevant to anything we can say about God." In Daniel Day Williams, "Suffering and Being in Empirical Theology," in *The Future of Empirical Theology,* pp. 191–192.

9. Ibid. p. 192

10. Quoted in John Coleman, "Power, the Powers and a Higher Power," in *CTSA*, Vol. 37 (New York, 1982) p. 3.

11. Ibid.

12. Ibid. pp. 4–5.

13. Dorothy Lee-Pollard, "Powerlessness as Power: A Key Emphasis in the Gospel of Mark," *Scottish Journal of Theology,* Vol. 40, 1987, p. 185.

14. Ibid.

15. Rollo May, *Power and Innocence* (New York: The Seabury Press, 1972) pp. 105–121.

16. Bernard Loomer in P.G. Sharpe Lectureship on Social Ethics. Quoted by J. Coleman, "Power, the Powers and a Higher Power," op. cit. p. 4.

17. Ibid. p. 5

18. "The use of the vocabulary of power in the context of social relationships is to speak of human agents, separately or together, in groups or organizations through action or inaction, significantly affecting the thoughts or action of others (specifically in a manner contrary to their interests). In speaking thus, one assumes that although the agents operate within structurally determined limits, they

nonetheless have a certain relative autonomy and could have acted differently. The future, thought is not entirely open, is not entirely closed either (and, indeed, the degree of openness is itself structurally determined)." In Steven Lukes, *Power: A Radical View* (New York: Macmillan, 1974) p. 86.

Index

Other Books in This Series